MAPPING MARYLAND

The Willard Hackerman Collection

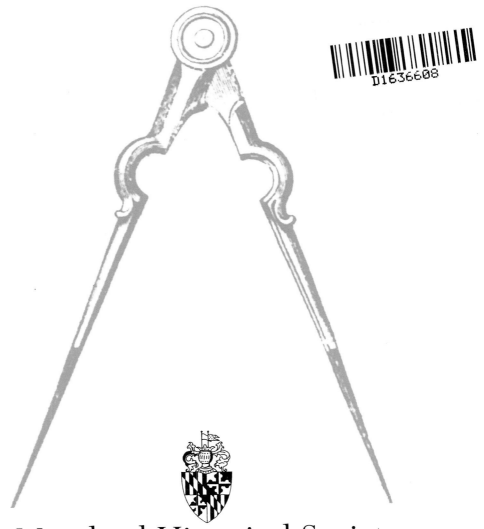

Maryland Historical Society

BALTIMORE, MARYLAND

Cartouche drawing from
"A Map of the most Inhabited part
of Virginia containing the whole
Province of Maryland with Part of
Pensilvania, New Jersey and
North Carolina"

Drawn by Joshua Fry & Peter Jefferson
in 1775.

(Figure 26.)

P of
ED part of

N I A

ROVINCE of

AND

of

ND NORTH CAROLINA

by

r Jefferson

Cover illustrations:
"A Map of Virginia and Maryland," 1676, by John Speed. (Fig. 14)
"The City of Baltimore," 1855, by Joseph Hutchins Colton. (Fig. 58)

An Introduction to Mapping

Maps evoke curiosity. We admire them and are intrigued by them. Who hasn't looked upon a map and dreamed of faraway places where we have never been or wish to go? Maps take us to lands both real and imaginary while we remain comfortably warm and free of the elements in our armchairs.

Maps can tell us where we have been, where we are, and where we are going. Historical maps are often studied to determine early boundaries, extinct place names, and various exploration routes. We also use maps to provide a spatial reference so that we know how far away we are from New York City or how close we are to the ocean or nearest wildlife sanctuary. Today's maps can be used to plan trips, to understand a city's complicated street network, and with the aid of computer mapping programs, to study the effects of pollution, population changes, and transportation development through the use of "what if" scenarios.

Maps have not always been produced with scientific methods, and our geographical knowledge has often included many unknowns. Can we imagine the trepidation, or love for adventure, that accompanied early explorers over mountains and across the oceans? Many maps were not produced by those explorers but were based on accounts of those trips and compiled by craftsmen who seldom ventured forth into the world.

It is hard to imagine a time without maps. They certainly represent one of the earliest forms of communication and were used in ancient Egypt, Greece, and Rome. Our understanding of Egyptian cartography reveals that they used maps for land surveying to redefine boundaries after the continuous flooding of the Nile. The Greeks made significant contributions to early cosmography with their theories of a spherical earth and their studies of its circumference. The Romans contributed early road maps as they mapped their empire. These early maps predate the printing arts and were created in manuscript form only. Some exist as clay tablets.

In the fifteenth century we begin to see the development of cartography as we know it. We have the rediscovery, at least in modern European terms, of Claudius Ptolemy's *Geography,* which was translated into Latin and the maps

redrawn ca. 1410, resulting in numerous manuscript editions. Not until 1477 was an edition with maps printed in Bologna. Ptolemy had published his original *Geography* ca. AD 150, and it continued to influence geography for over 1,000 years.

The sixteenth century brought a refinement and a science to the art of mapmaking. Nowhere is this more obvious than in the works of Abraham Ortelius and Gerard Mercator. The early sixteenth century saw the publication of many separate regional maps in Italy, the Low Countries, and Germany. Ortelius, as a map dealer, was aware of these maps and used them to create what many consider the first true atlas of maps, the *Theatrum orbis terrarum* in 1570. Mercator, a friend of Ortelius, was also at work making maps. He published his famous world map of 1569 as well as maps of Flanders, the British Isles, and Europe and a pair of globes. The sixteenth century introduced the American continent to cartography, and its delineation continued to evolve through a century of great exploration.

The seventeenth century was dominated by the Golden Age of Dutch Cartography; however, the four great powers—England, Spain, France, and the Netherlands—all contributed to the development of cartography and further exploration of the Americas. Successful English settlement began in 1607 at Jamestown and resulted in John Smith's significant map of Virginia. The French were led into Canada by Champlain's explorations and his spectacular cartography. Manuscript maps in Dutch and Spanish archives reveal that each country was sailing the East Coast of America in the early seventeenth century. Blaeu and Jansson soon published the results of these voyages in the great Dutch atlases. The seventeenth century also produced one of the most accurate maps of the Americas, the Herrman map of Virginia and Maryland.

The eighteenth century may best be described as one of definition for the American continent. European mapmakers continued to learn more of the interior and published detailed maps of the East Coast. Delisle's *Carte de la Louisiane et du Cours du Mississipi* reveals the expanse of the Mississippi Valley and is the first to accurately map the Mississippi Delta region. This century, while still dominated by European mapmakers, introduced a larger number of American cartographers as well as detailed regional maps, i.e. Fry & Jefferson's *A Map of the Most Inhabited part of Virginia . . . ,* Evans's *Middle British Colonies,* and Scull's *Pennsylvania.* The colonies were more accurately defined with large maps such as Mitchell's *A Map of the British and French Dominions in North America* and with detailed maps such as Bonner's *The Town of Boston* and Scull and Heap's *A Map of Philadelphia.* The end of this century reveals the rise of industrious American mapmakers, and Dennis Griffith's *Map of Maryland* is a good example.

The nineteenth century is truly the century of American mapmaking and witnessed exponential growth in the number of individuals and firms producing maps of a new nation. The need for updated maps to record territorial expansion, roadbuilding, and the construction of railways was to be met by this growing commercial industry. Familiar names such as Lucas, Lewis, Melish, Reid, Morse, and the later Coltons and Mitchells dominated mapmaking in this country and produced separate maps and atlases in large numbers. The latter part of the century witnessed an interest in large-scale mapping and created the county land ownership atlas business and the fire insurance maps and atlases that have also become collector's items.

The twentieth century has seen significant contributions as well. Road maps began to flourish, though today early road maps are valuable rarities. As we approach a new millenium, more maps are produced using digital technology, as computers store a myriad of data to be called back on demand. Will these maps be studied and viewed with similar mystery?

This wonderful exhibit and its accompanying catalog provide windows to the past so that we may look back in time and view the evolution of a New World from its adventurous explorers and their beautiful maps.

DAVID COBB
Head of the Map Collection
Harvard University

March 1998

An Overview of Maryland Mapping

Marylanders possess a centuries-old interest in map collecting. In February 1763, William Rind set up a private circulating library in Annapolis that included a selection of maps. According to Rind, "as the richest Soil, without due cultivation, runs into rank and unprofitable Weeds, so little Fruit can be expected from the best natural Endowments, where the Mind is not under the Direction of proper intellectual Aids." Unfortunately, the subscription-funded enterprise failed to garner the necessary financial support, and it appears that Rind's map collection was dispersed in the summer of 1764.

In 1844 a more successful attempt to organize a permanent map collection was made when several enlightened gentlemen of business founded the Maryland Historical Society Library. The organization's collecting policy "deemed it advisable to annex . . . Topographical descriptions of towns, cities, counties or states, with maps." An initial donation of two maps, one of the C&O Canal and another of Florida, served as the nucleus of a valuable reference collection.

Continuing in this tradition of map collecting are the twentieth-century efforts of Willard Hackerman, a Baltimore businessman and philanthropist who has amassed in the remarkably short space of fifteen years one of the finest collections of Maryland-related printed maps. In his engineering career and in his current position as president and chief executive officer of the Whiting-Turner Contracting Company, the practical use of maps has been an integral part of Hackerman's everyday life. Yet, over time practical necessity and applications gave way to an interest in Maryland's past and the engraver's art, prompting him to collect historical maps. The many fruits of Hackerman's collecting can be viewed publicly for the first time in the exhibition *Mapping Maryland: The Willard Hackerman Collection.*

This fine collection of over seventy maps, many hand-colored, provides the means by which to trace chronologically the graphic depiction of the state from its pre-colonial period through the mid-nineteenth century. The *Mapping Maryland* exhibition, which contains almost all of the collec-

tion, also features a fine representation of Maryland-related navigational and general regional maps.

The mapping of Maryland developed over several centuries and involved the contributions of many cartographers. John White's 1590 map of Virginia (fig. 1) hints at a vast estuary bearing the name "Chesepiooc Sinus," whose source appears to spring forth from beneath the title cartouche, marking the first appearance of the name "Chesapeake Bay" on any map. White's map, however, was soon superseded by that of Captain John Smith of Jamestown. Smith's meticulous 1608–9 survey of the bay region, encompassing some 2,000 miles of coast in all, served as the intellectual foundation for a map referred to by cartographers for over sixty years. Printed in 1612, the Smith map (fig. 3) became the "Mother map" or prototype for numerous derivatives and an inspiration for later regional depictions (figs. 4, 5, 6, 11, 14, 22).

Cartographers often "borrowed" ideas and images in their entirety. Willem Blaeu, the famed Dutch cartographer and printer, appears to have wholly appropriated Smith's design yet gives it a more refined and elegant interpretation in his 1630 *Nova Virginia Tabula,* (fig. 5). Johann Baptist Homann, a noted German mapmaker, adapted Smith's rendition of the Susquehannock warrior for his own cartouche design in his 1714 *Virginia Marylandia et Carolina* (fig. 18).

The next major influence in the cartography of Maryland came with the work of Augustine Herrman. Herrman, a Bohemian immigrant, negotiated an agreement with Lord Baltimore to produce a map of Maryland in exchange for a land grant. Begun in 1659 and requiring years of surveys and information gathering, the 1673 map (fig. 12) would determine the depiction of Maryland for eighty years. Herrman's influence is seen immediately in the sea charts of van Keulen (1684) and Mortier (1696) (figs. 16, 17). Numerous maps created during the first half of the 1700s continued to borrow from Herrman (figs. 21, 23, 25).

It was not until the eighteenth century that the portrayal of Maryland in maps began to resemble what we know today. With the exception of navigational charts, mapmakers abandoned John Smith's orientation of placing North to the right. Also, until the eighteenth century, what little was known of the western region had been drawn largely from oral information supplied by Native Americans or frontiersmen, resulting in sketchy and sometimes imaginative interpretations. The 1751 map by Joshua Fry and Peter Jefferson provides an early, if broad, portrayal of the panhandle area of the colony (fig. 26). Yet not until 1769, when the king and his council ratified the Mason-Dixon survey line, could cartographers place Maryland's northern border with certainty.

In 1795, with the work of Dennis Griffith (fig. 41), Maryland mapmaking reached its eighteenth-century zenith. After he had spent several years producing this topographically accurate, highly detailed work, Griffith found that his map attracted few buyers, and he died bankrupt. Griffith's legacy, however, can easily be seen in later works (figs. 46, 50, 56).

Printed Maryland city maps first appeared in the late eighteenth century. Baltimore, as a population center, served as a natural subject for mapmakers. Two French cartographers produced the first detailed maps during the 1790s. A. P. Folie (fig. 40) and Charles Varlé (fig. 44) both present the early city and its three distinct yet rapidly encroaching, areas: Baltimore, Old Town, and Fell's Point. Another early map, this one with Baltimore inset within a map of Maryland, came from the hand of Fielding Lucas Jr. Originally featured within Lucas's *Cabinet Atlas* of 1824, this work is distinct in that it was the first map of a city in any world atlas (fig. 46). Thomas Poppleton's 1822 plan of Baltimore is the marriage of practicality and art and combines civic propaganda with decoration (fig. 49). Harkening to the tradition of some earlier cartographers, a series of beautifully executed vignettes surround the map. Featuring prominent city buildings and their individual construction costs, the engravings boast the municipal achievements of what was then America's third largest city.

Navigational charts form a portion of the Hackerman collection. Reliable information on the Chesapeake Bay and the Atlantic coast was essential in an area whose early economy, and even at times its very existence, were determined by water. Sir Robert Dudley's extremely rare 1646 *Carta Particolare della Virginia,* based on the Mercator projection,

was contained in his sea atlas *Dell Arcano del Mare,* the first such atlas produced by an Englishman (fig. 9). Dudley, a Roman Catholic, fled religious persecution in England and settled in Tuscany, thus his work appears with Italian annotations. The John Mount and Thomas Page chart of 1745–58, derived from one that had appeared five decades earlier, contains numerous depth sounding notations throughout its field (fig. 24). The upper Chesapeake is highlighted in the work of C. P. Hauducoeur (fig. 43), whose beautifully engraved 1799 chart also contains an inset plan of Havre de Grace.

The Hackerman collection also includes a selection of maps of Maryland set within the context of its neighbors. These more general maps are important in the development of the cartography of the region. It is also amusing to note occasional misinterpretations. Dudley's 1646 *Carta Secunda Generale de America* is an early, somewhat sketchy, view of the East Coast that features a vastly wide Chesapeake Bay (fig. 10). An imaginative view of the Southeast is contained in Homann's 1714 map: Florida's panhandle appears to "circle around" the other southern colonies and head so far north as to almost share a border with Maryland (fig. 18).

The serious collecting of maps can be arduous, time-consuming, and expensive. As with all collecting, there is always some other version or edition desired; amassing never ends. The true value in collecting, however, is the ability to share your efforts with others. With *Mapping Maryland: The Willard Hackerman Collection,* a generous and knowledgeable collector has given the public a wonderful opportunity to study and appreciate early cartography. He has made it possible to better understand our past, and thereby ourselves.

We would like to extend special gratitude to Mr. Ronald Grim, specialist in cartographic history, Geography and Map Division, Library of Congress, for his time and invaluable advice.

R O B E R T W. S C H O E B E R L E I N
Curator of Prints and Photographs
Maryland Historical Society Library

March 1998

1. JOHN WHITE, *Americae Pars / Nunc Virginia*, 1590

   (See color plate on page 17.)

2. ABRAHAM ORTELIUS, *Map of the Roman Empire*, 1601

   Abraham Ortel (1527–98), better known by the Latinized version of his last name, Ortelius, began his career as map colorist and seller. By the 1560s, he had achieved sufficient skill to enable him to prepare his own maps for publication. In 1570 Ortelius published his masterwork, *Theatrum Orbis Terrarum,* which is considered the first modern atlas and appeared in forty-two editions. This map, which appeared in the 1601 Latin edition of the *Theatrum,* depicts the realm of Ancient Rome.

3. JOHN SMITH, *Virginia*, 1608 [1612]

This map contains the first detailed delineation of the area to be known as "Maryland." Serving as a "Mother map," Smith's work spawned nine major derivatives and provided inspiration for subsequent regional maps until superseded in 1673. The map was noted for its accuracy, and archeologists referred to it to locate Maryland's Native American settlements.

4. THEODORE DE BRY, *Virginia*, 1628

This German language version produced by de Bry for his book, *Dreyzehender Thiel Americae,* is the third derivative from John Smith's map.

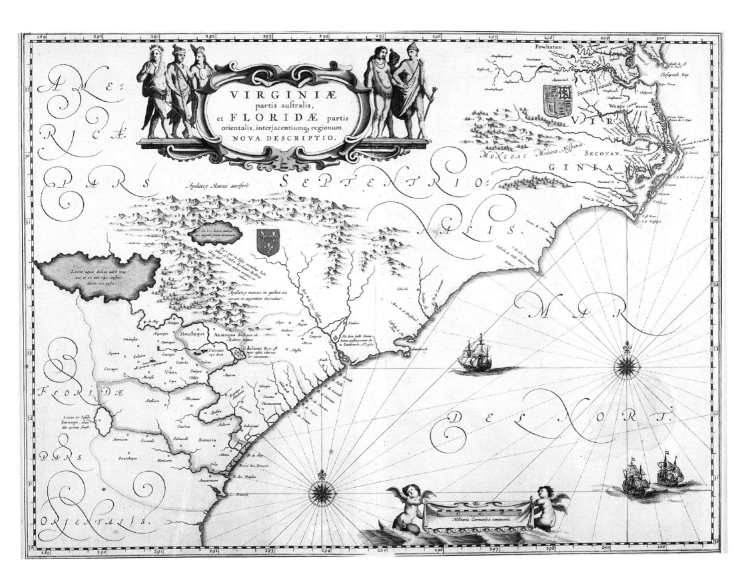

5. WILLEM BLAEU, *Nova Virginae Tabula*, 1630 [1640] (second state)

(See color plate on page 18.)

6. HENRY HONDIUS, *Nova Virginae Tabula*, 1633

(See color plate on page 18.)

7. JOHN OGILBY, *Noua Terrae-Mariae tabula*, 1635 [1671]

(See color plate on page 19.)

8. WILLEM BLAEU, *Virginae partis australis, et Floridae*, 1638 [1641]

The work of Willem Blaeu, the most notable Dutch cartographer of the seventeenth century is known for its accuracy and high aesthetic value. Note that the Chesapeake Bay has evolved from a small bay to its proper size as a large estuary.

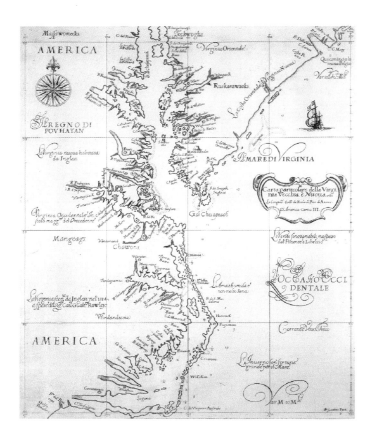

9. SIR ROBERT DUDLEY, *Carta particolare della Virginia Vecchia e Nuoua*, 1646

Sir Robert Dudley, an expatriate Englishman living in Italy, produced the first marine atlas to use the Mercator projection for the basis of its maps. Taken from Dudley's rare first edition of his 1646 *Dell Arcano del Mare*, this version's title cartouche lacks the page number found in the 1661 second printing.

10. SIR ROBERT DUDLEY, *Carta secunda Generale del America*, 1646

This is a regional map of the southeast coast of America from Dudley's 1646 edition of the *Arcano*. It took engraver Antonio Franceso Lucini eight years to complete the copperplates of the charts included in this atlas.

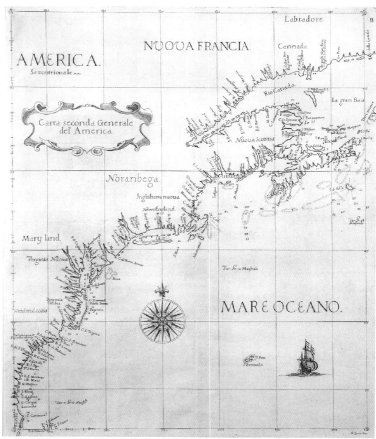

11. JOHN OGILBY, *Nova Virginae Tabula*, 1671

This map is the eighth derivative of John Smith's *Virginia*. It is a careful copy of the 1633 Hondius map on the same subject. Ogilby included this work in his *America*.

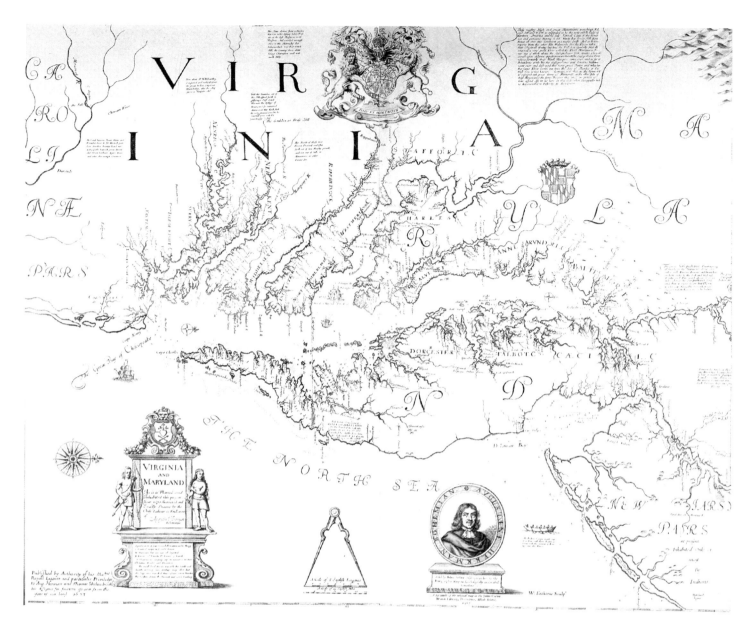

12. AUGUSTINE HERRMAN, *Virginia and Maryland as it is planted and inhabited this present year 1670*, 1673 (reproduction)

Herrman's map served as the prototype for subsequent Maryland maps well into the eighteenth century. Its large size may have contributed to its present-day scarcity; only six copies have been located worldwide.

13. RICHARD BLOME, *A Draught of the Sea Coast and Rivers of Virginia, Maryland, and New England*, c. 1675

Despite the availability of Augustine Herrman's map, Blome produced this rough version largely based upon the earlier work of Ogilby. An English cartographer and publisher, Blome produced maps on English counties, British possessions, and the world in the late seventeenth century.

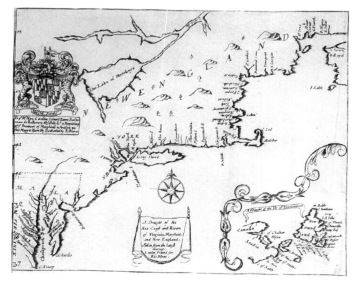

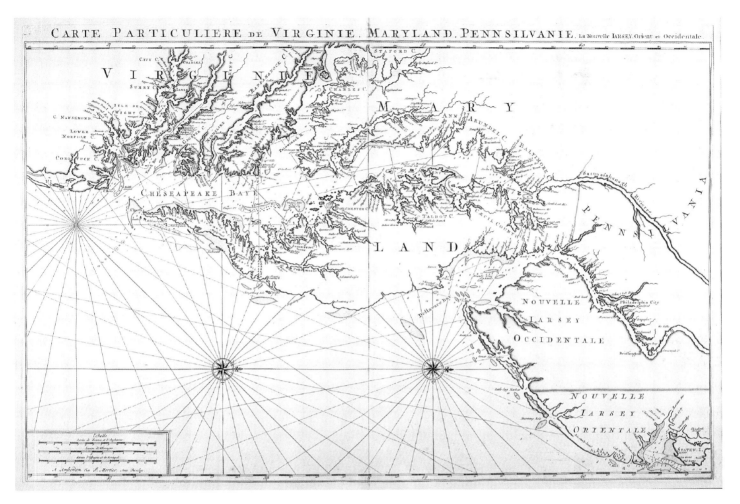

CARTE PARTICULIERE DE VIRGINIE. MARYLAND. PENNSILVANIE. La Nouvelle IARSEY.Orient et Occidentale

14. JOHN SPEED, *A Map of Virginia and Maryland*, 1676 (first state)

(See color plate on page 20.)

15. ALLAIN MANESSON MALLET, *Virginie*, 1683

(See color plate on page 20.)

16. JOHANNES VAN KEULEN, *Pas Kaart van de Zee Kusten van Virginia*, 1684

(See color plate on page 21.)

17. PIERRE MORTIER, *Carte Particuliere de Virginie, Maryland, Pennsilvanie, La Nouvelle Iarsey Orient et Occidentale*, 1696

This map, published by Mortier, came from the hand of Alexis Hubert Jaillot (c.1632–1712). Trained originally as a sculptor, Jaillot often fully colored his maps and sometimes illuminated them with gold.

19. HENRI A. CHATELAIN, *Nouvelle Carte . . . Pensylvanie, Maryland . . . Nouvelle Iarsey*, 1719

Chatelain (1684–1743), a geographer and publisher, produced this map for inclusion in his *Atlas Historique*.

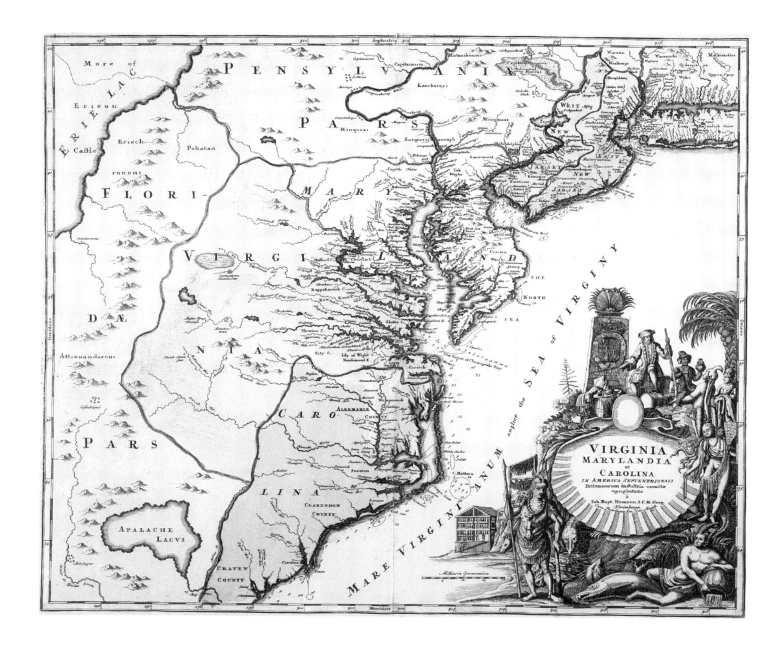

18. JOHANN BAPTIST HOMANN, *Virginia, Marylandia,
et Carolina*, 1714 [1740]

Homann, the geographer to the king of the Holy
Roman Empire, led his contemporaries in coloring
his maps, although he usually left the cartouche
area untouched. This map, which contains some
fanciful and erroneous information, served to pro-
mote the emigration of Germans to America.

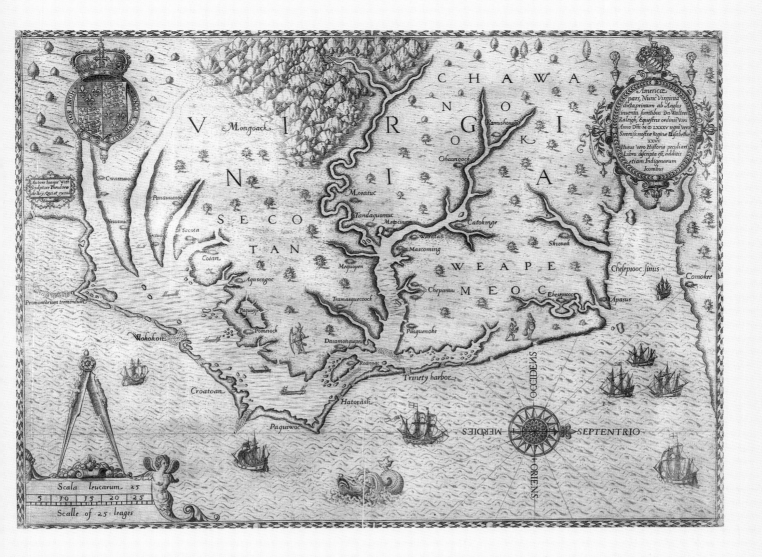

1. JOHN WHITE, *Americae Pars / Nunc Virginia*, 1590

John White's map, although it portrays a minute portion of Maryland, is significant for the many firsts it contributed to the mapping of the region. The name "Chesapeake Bay" (Chesepiooc Sinus) makes its initial appearance. White's map also served as a prototype for several successive area maps until the early seventeenth century.

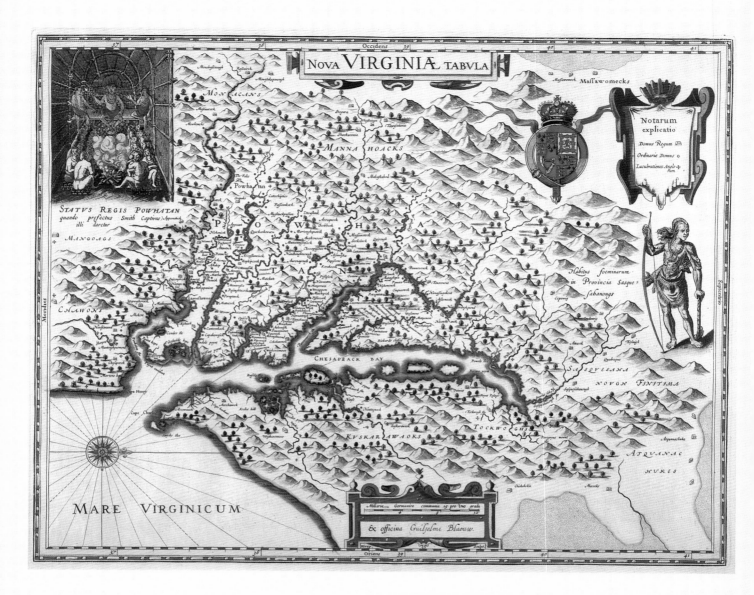

5. WILLEM BLAEU, *Nova Virginae Tabula*, 1630 [1640] (second state)

   More refined in its interpretation, this map is the first in a series of nine derived from John Smith's *Virginia*.

6. HENRY HONDIUS, *Nova Virginae Tabula*, 1633

   This is the fifth derivative from Smith's map. Henry Hondius, son of the famed Dutch cartographer Jodocus Hondius, continued to operate his family's business until his death in 1657.

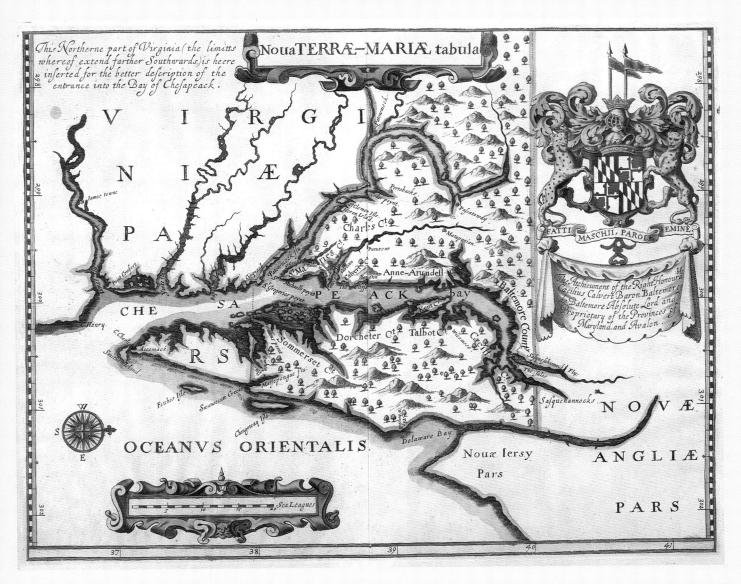

7. JOHN OGILBY, *Noua Terrae-Mariae tabula*, 1635
[1671]

This is a second edition of what popularly is
called the *Lord Baltimore Map,* which first appeared
in Father Andrew White's *A Relation of Maryland*, a
1635 publication devised to entice colonists to
the province. John Ogilby, a one-time "dancing-
master," produced this map for his illustrated
atlas, *America*.

14. JOHN SPEED, *A Map of Virginia and Maryland*, 1676
(first state)

Speed included this work, the ninth and last major
derivative of Smith's map, in his *Theatre of the
Empire*. It is an important map since its reflects
new information published by Augustine Herrman
some three years earlier.

15. ALLAIN MANESSON MALLET, *Virginie*, 1683

Mallet, an engineer in the service of Louis XIV,
produced this map for inclusion in his five-volume
Description de L'Univers.

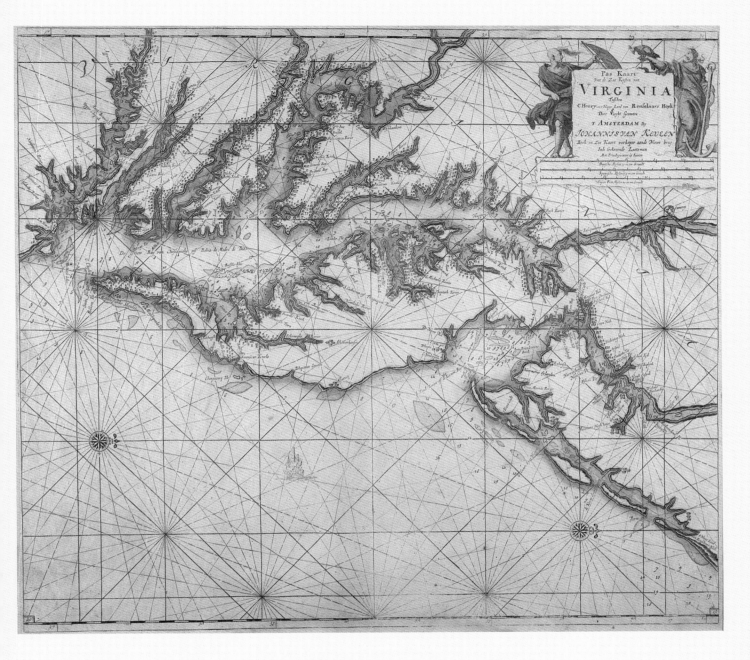

16. JOHANNES VAN KEULEN, *Pas Kaart van de Zee Kusten van Virginia*, 1684

This is an example of a hydrographic chart, which features little information on coastal areas except for town names. Van Keulen produced a sea atlas, *De Goote Nieuwe Zee-Atlas,* which incorporated a series of American coastal maps, works freely copied by later map-makers. The van Keulens were the premier publishers of nautical works in the late seventeenth century.

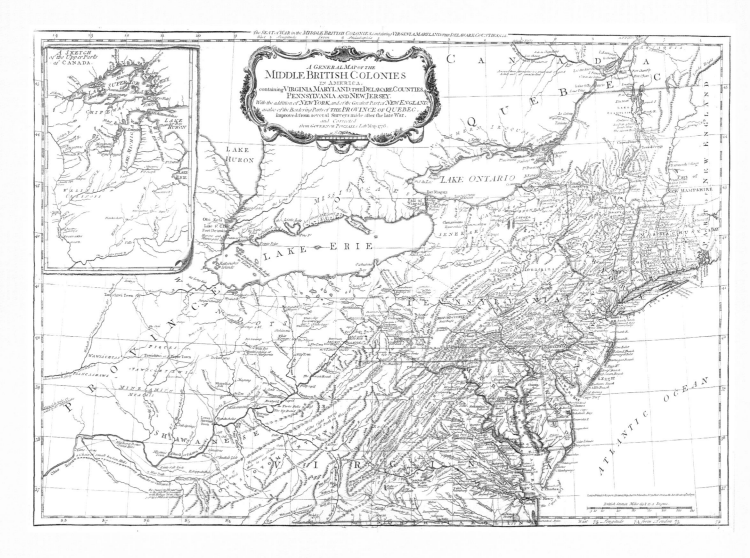

32. ROBERT SAYER & JOHN BENNET, *A General Map of the British Middle Colonies*, 1776

Bennett (d.1787) joined with Sayer (1725–94) to form a London publishing house in 1770. One of their works, the *American Military Pocket Atlas,* was intended as a field reference guide for British military officers during the Revolutionary War. This map is one of six featured in the *Atlas.*

33. GEORGES-LOUIS LE ROUGE, *Virginie, Maryland, en 2 feuilles par Fry et Jefferson*, 1777

Educated as a military engineer, Le Rouge (fl. 1740–80) became a publisher of atlases and offered some of the finest French-made maps relating to North America. This reduced version of the Fry-Jefferson map is typical of his work.

Following spread:

26. JOSHUA FRY & PETER JEFFERSON, *A Map of the most inhabited part of Virginia, containing the whole province of Maryland, with part of Pensilvania, New Jersey and North Carolina.* 1751 [1775]

Fry and Jefferson completed an extensive survey of Virginia to produce this important map. Though the western part of Maryland lacks detail, this map is the first to accurately represent the parallel ridges of the Appalachian mountains. This 1775 impression of the 1751 first edition differs little from the original with the exception of the date found within the decorative cartouche, and some additional place-names.

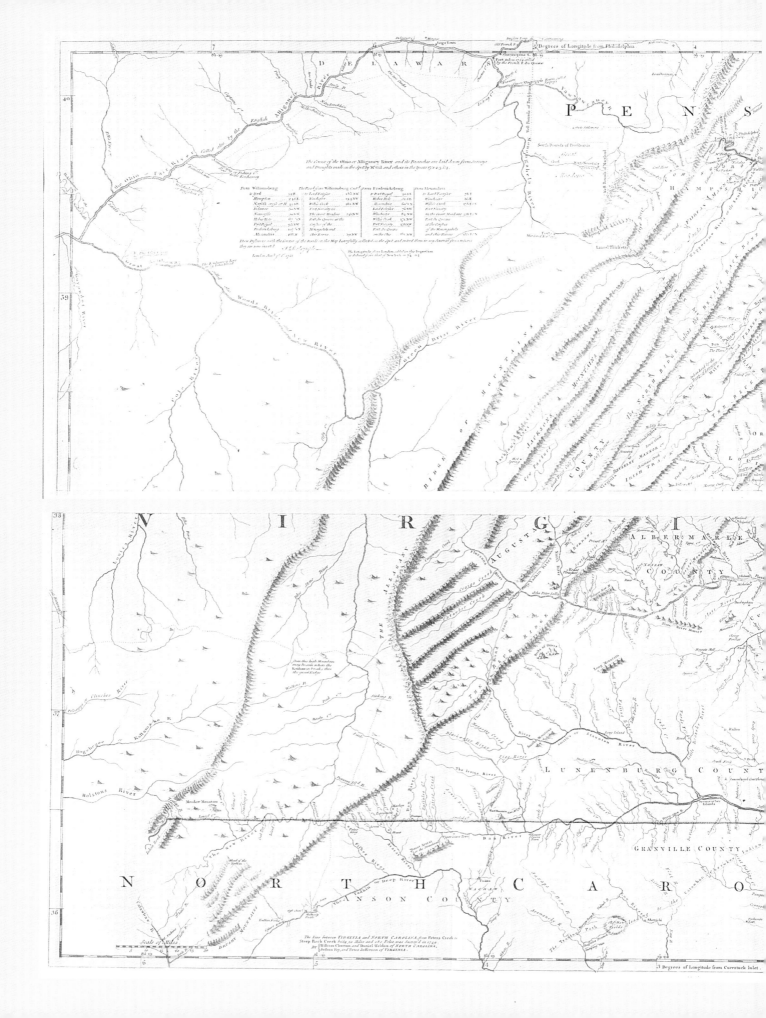

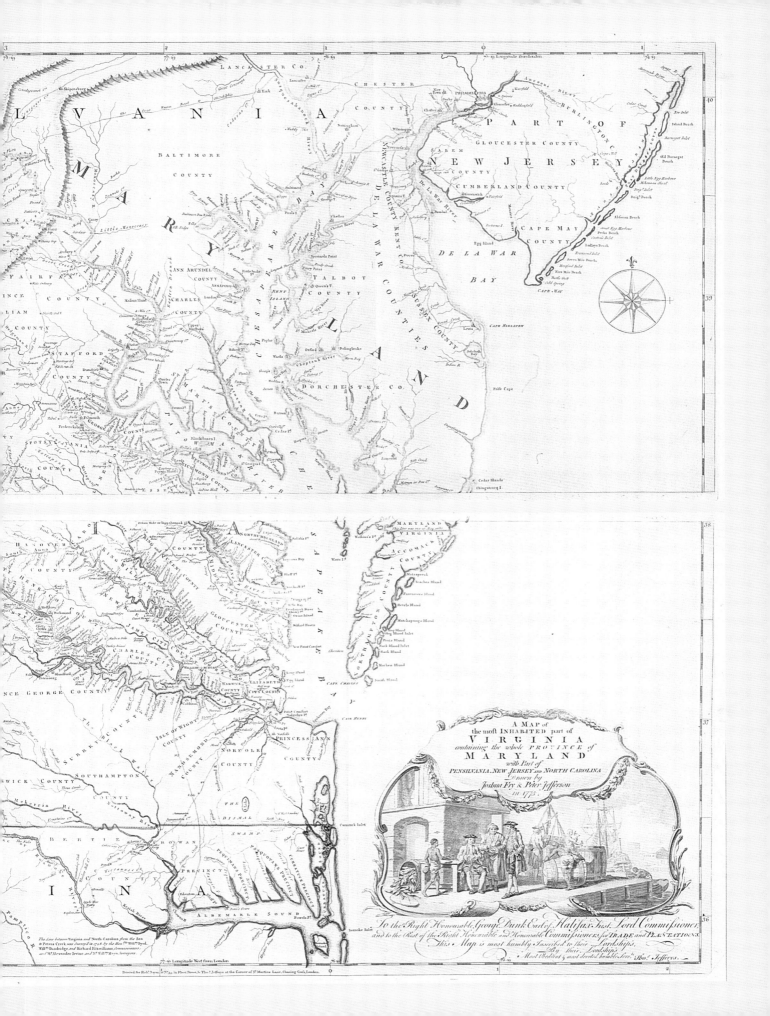

A MAP of
the most INHABITED part of
VIRGINIA
containing the whole PROVINCE of
MARYLAND
with Part of
PENSILVANIA, NEW JERSEY and NORTH CAROLINA
Drawn by
Joshua Fry & Peter Jefferson
in 1775.

To the Right Honourable, George Dunk Earl of Halifax, First Lord Commissioner, and to the Rest of the Right Honourable and Honourable Commissioners, for TRADE and PLANTATIONS. This Map is most humbly Inscribed to their Lordships, By their Lordships, Most Obedient & most devoted humble Servt. Thos. Jefferys.

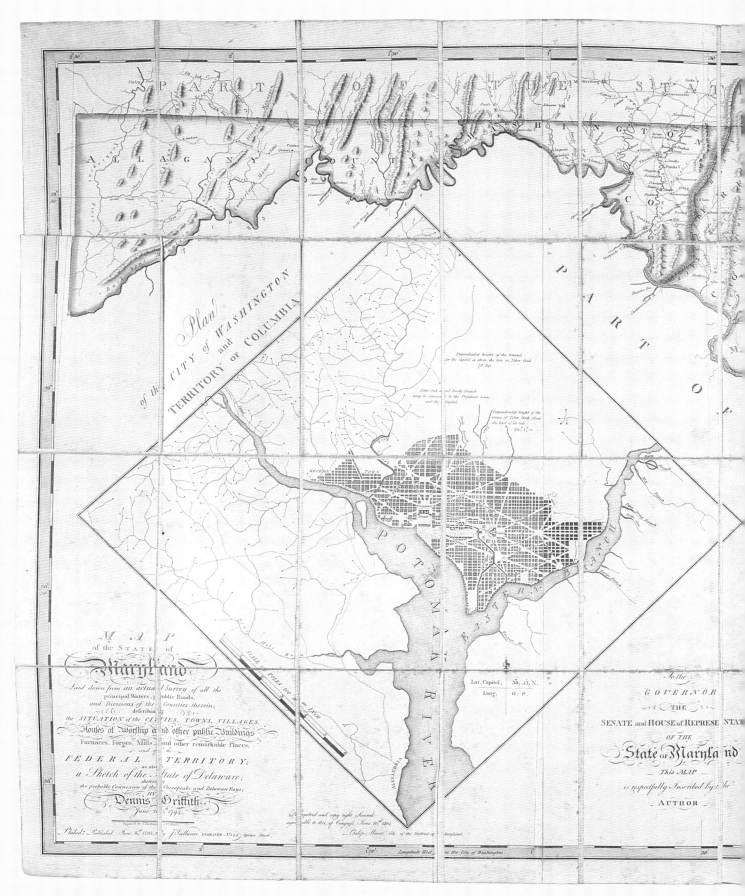

41. DENNIS GRIFFITH, *Map of the State of Maryland*, 1794 [1795]

...iffith, a surveyor, produced this accurate map of Maryland, which is considered the finest eighteenth-century map of the state. ...refully executed and containing many topographical details, Griffith's map was an achievement for its time and is considered the ...t official state map.

27

49.

THOMAS H. POPPLETON,
Plan of the City of Baltimore,
1822 [1852]

T. H. Poppleton, described
in an 1811 issue of the
*Federal Gazette and Baltimore
Daily Advertiser* as a
"Practical Land Surveyor
and Draughtsman," initiated
a survey of the city in 1812.
Not until February 1816,
however, did the Maryland
General Assembly commis-
sion the cartographer to
print the map. Though not
a financially lucrative ven-
ture at its first issue,
Poppleton's work under-
went subsequent modifica-
tions and printings and
served as the reference for
Baltimore's physical development until the 1880s.

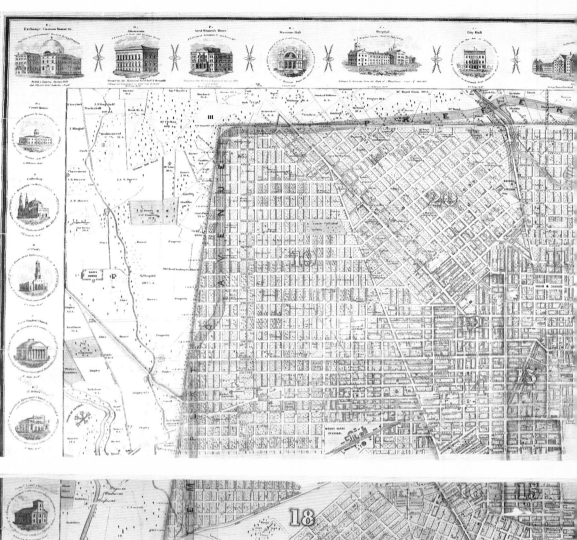

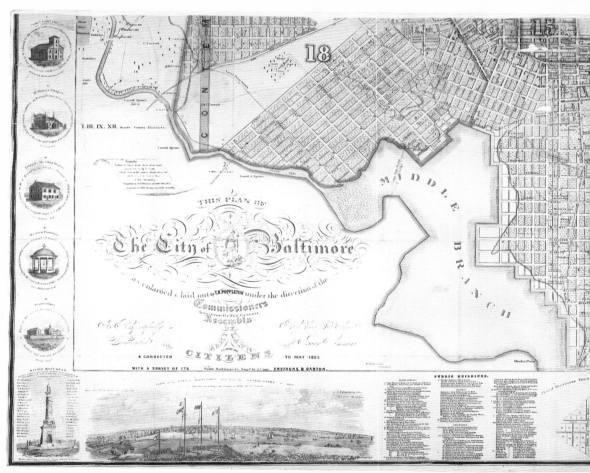

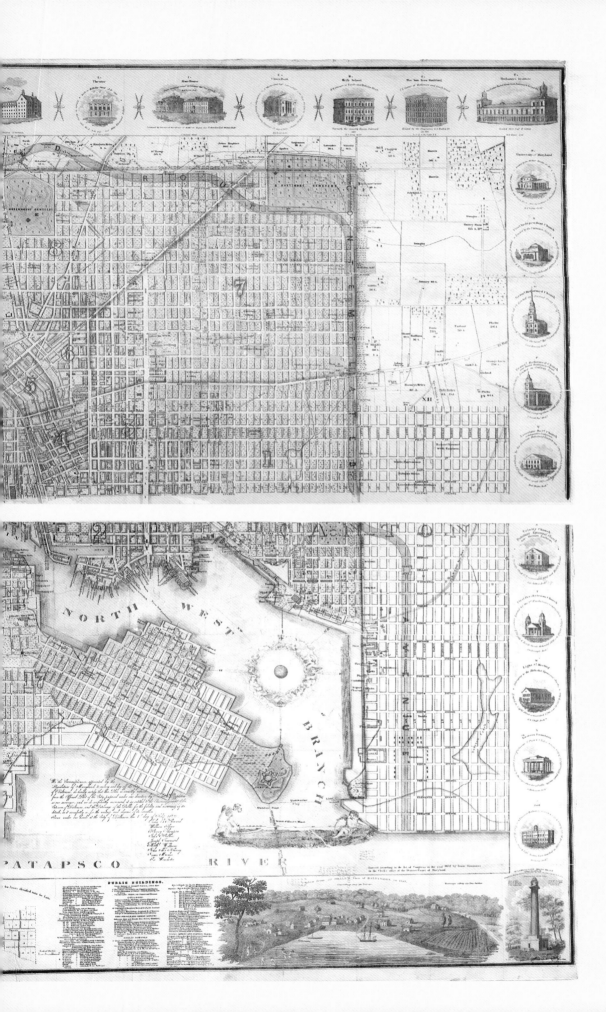

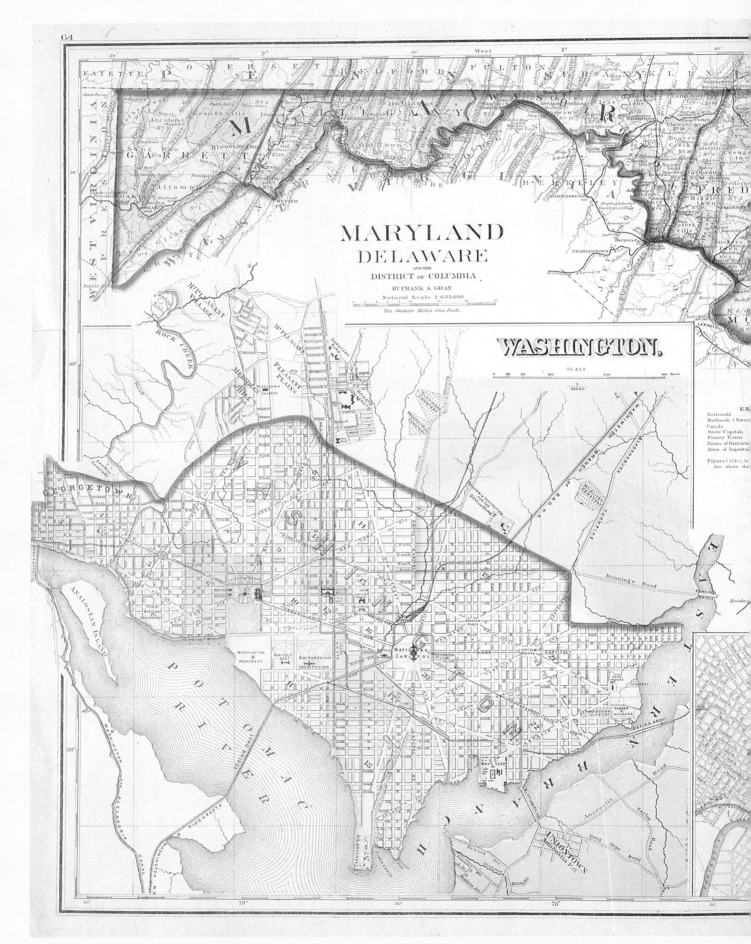

61. O. W. GRAY & SON, *Gray's New Map of Maryland*, 1876

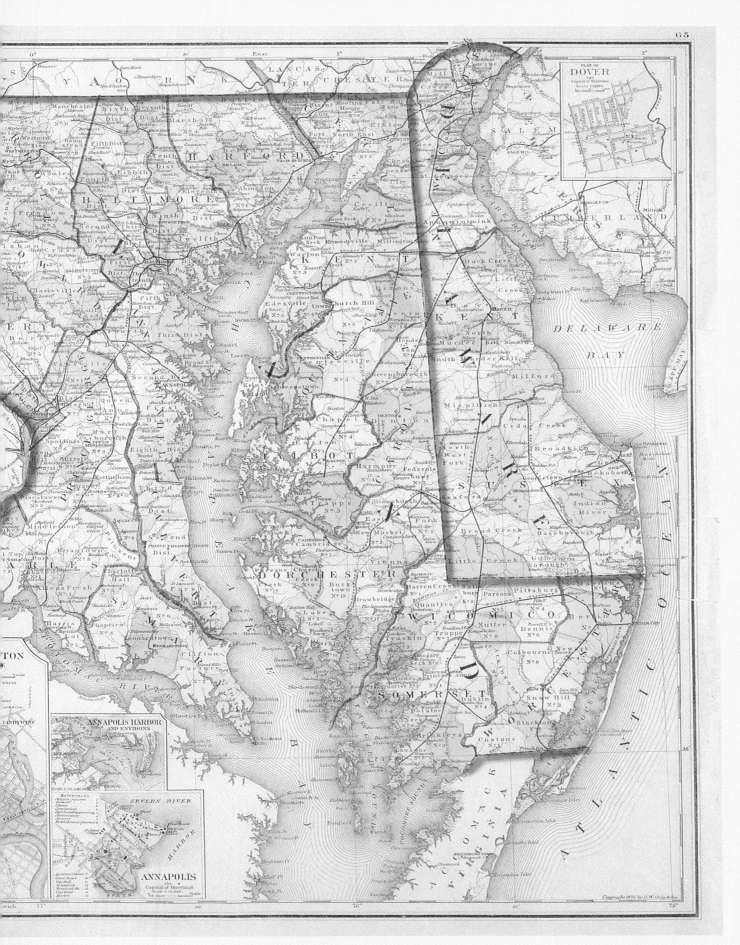

Philadelphia-based firm produced this map for inclusion within an atlas.

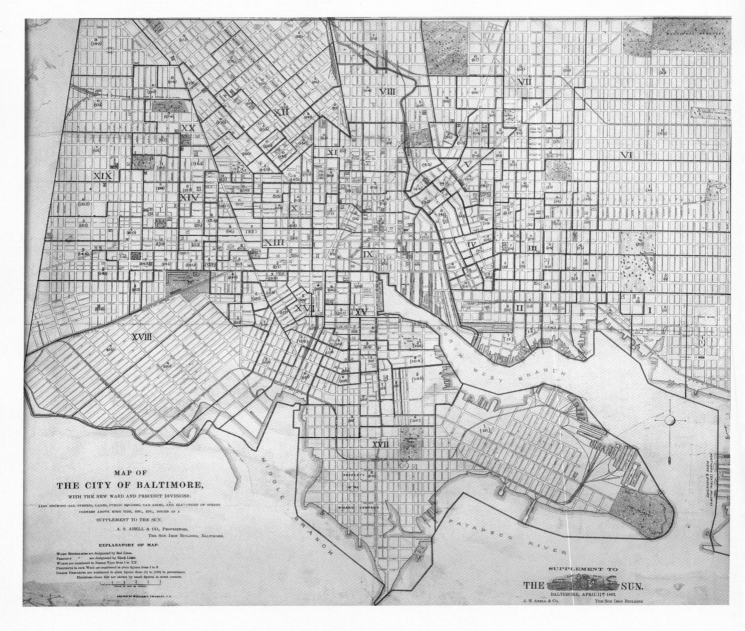

62. WILLIAM P. TWAMLEY [for the *Baltimore Sun*],
Map of the City of Baltimore, 1882

Produced as a supplement for the *Baltimore Sun*
newspaper, this map depicts Baltimore's rapid
growth northward during the post–Civil War era.

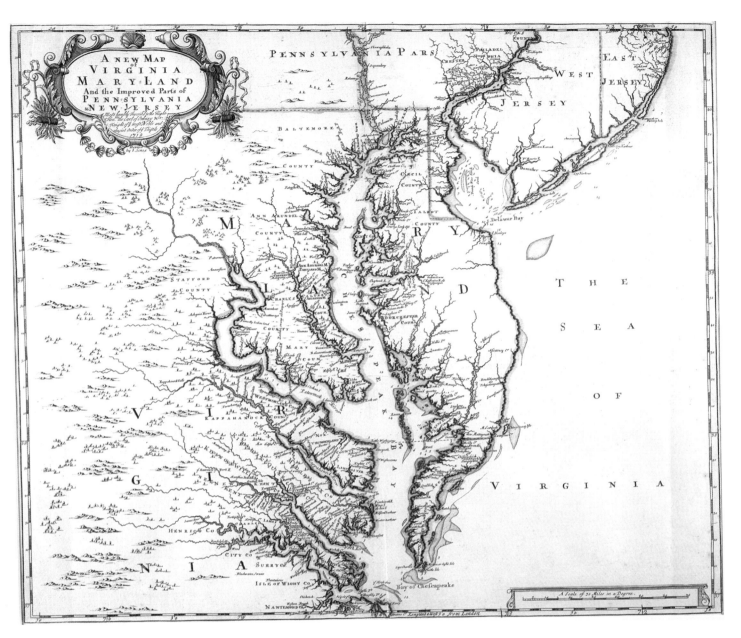

20. JOHN SENEX, *A New Map of Virginia, Maryland and the Improved Parts of Pennsylvania & New Jersey*, 1719

From *A New General Atlas (1721)*, John Senex's (fl. 1703–46) maps broadly document the British Empire's holdings in the New World. While serving as the geographer for Queen Anne, Senex produced a map in 1732 that was used in negotiating the Maryland-Pennsylvania border dispute.

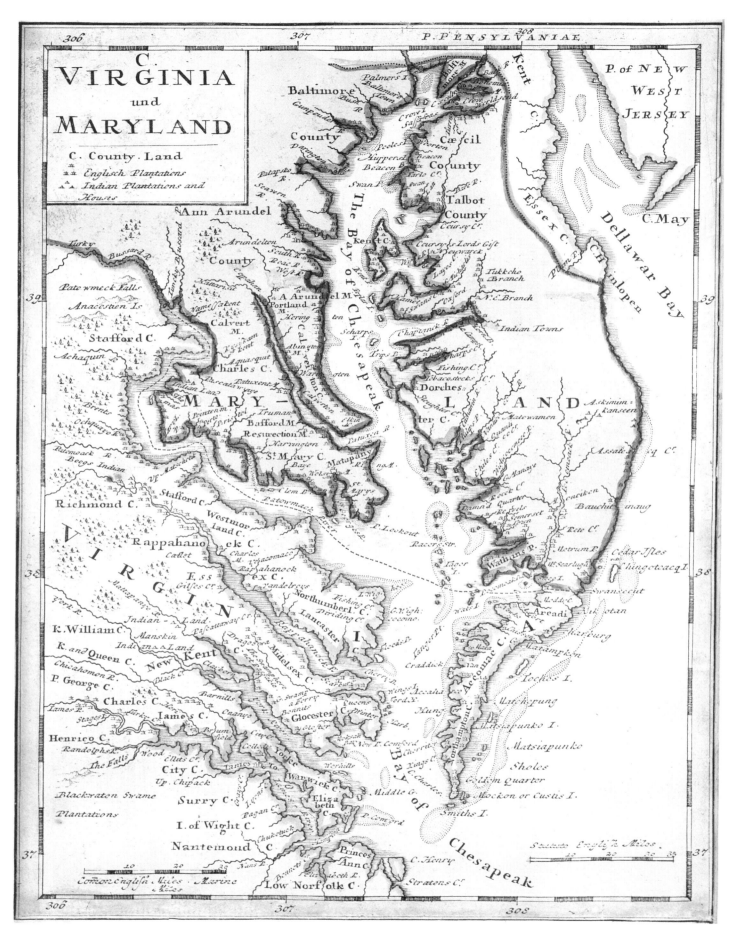

C.
VIRGINIA
und
MARYLAND

C. County. Land
✳✳ Englisch Plantations
△△ Indian Plantations and
Houses

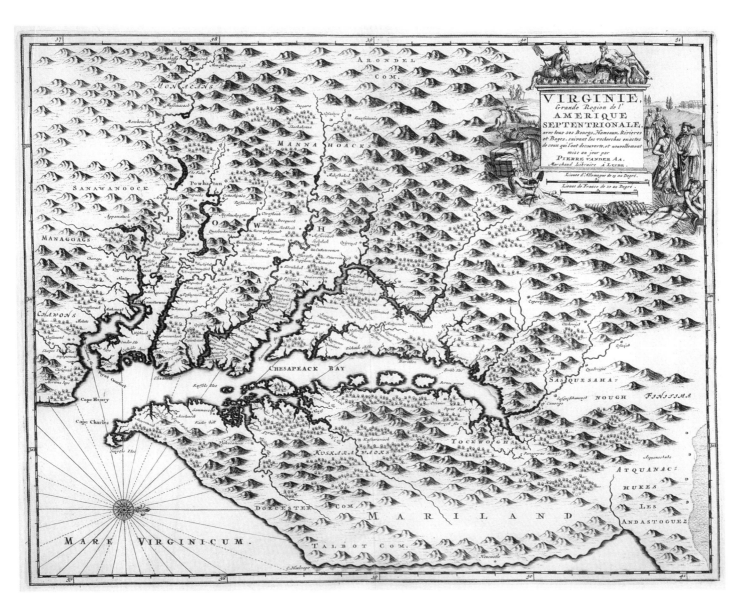

21. JOHANN BAPTIST HOMANN, *Virginia und Maryland*, 1719

The patriarch of a family of notable eighteenth-century German cartographers, Johann Baptist Homann (1663–1724) produced this version of the widely copied map first executed in 1708 by Herman Moll.

22. PIETER VAN DER AA, *Virginie*, 1729

To produce this map, Dutch cartographer van der Aa acquired the copperplate for John Ogilby's 1671 map *Nova Virginae Tabula* and altered it, incorporating three new counties in Maryland.

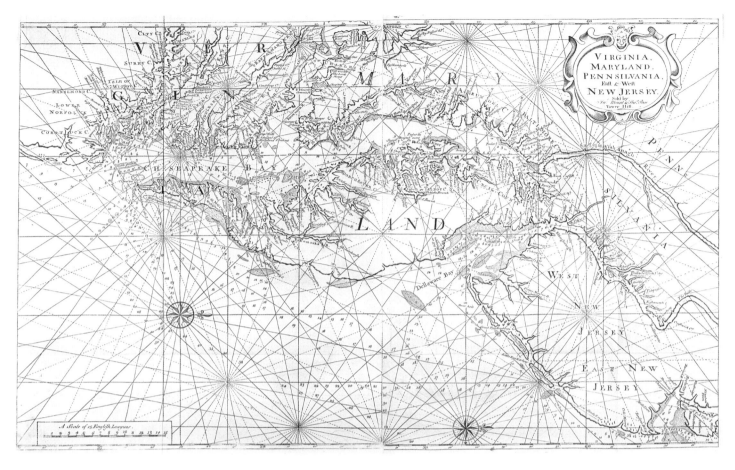

(right)

23. HERMAN MOLL, *Virginia and Maryland*, 1736

   Moll, a Dutch cartographer residing in London, produced numerous maps and atlases bearing decorative cartouches and vignettes until his death in 1732. This 1736 map is a reprint of his original work first featured in 1708 within Oldmixon's *British Empire in America*.

(above)

24. JOHN MOUNT & THOMAS PAGE, *Virginia, Maryland… New Jersey*, 1743–70

   Mount and Page, a London-based publishing house, produced this map for a later edition of the important 1689 sea atlas, *The English Pilot*.

(opposite)

25. EMANUEL BOWEN, *A New and Accurate Map of Virginia & Maryland*, 1747 [1752]

   An engraver of maps to both George II and Louis XV, Bowen produced this version of Herman Moll's 1708 map for his *Complete System of Geography*.

36

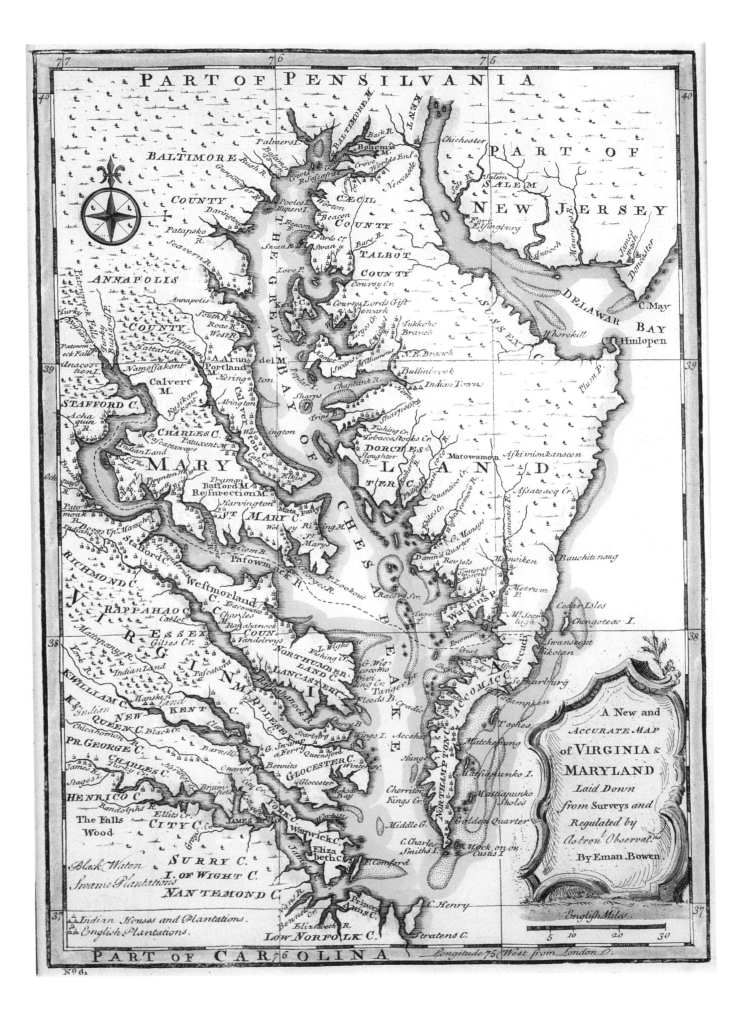

A New and
ACCURATE MAP
of VIRGINIA &
MARYLAND
Laid Down
from Surveys and
Regulated by
Astron.l Observat.ns
By Eman. Bowen

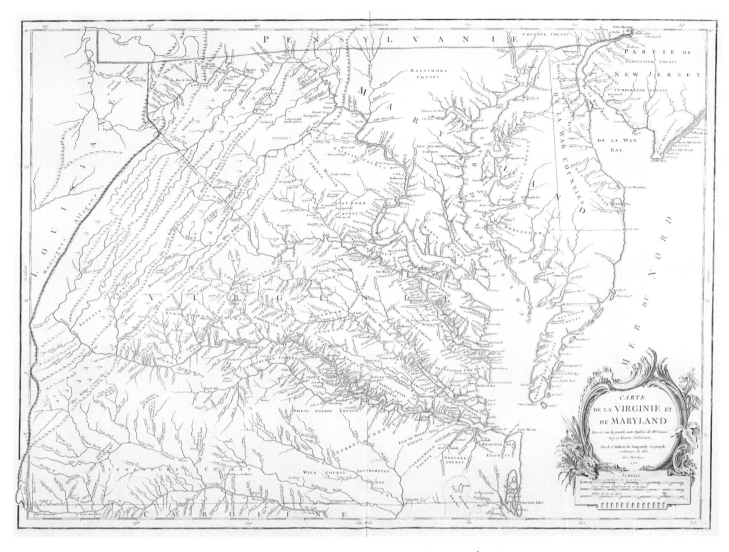

26. JOSHUA FRY & PETER JEFFERSON, *A Map of the most inhabited part of Virginia, containing the whole province of Maryland, with part of Pensilvania, New Jersey and North Carolina.* 1751 [1775]

(See color plate on pages 24 and 25.)

(above)

27. DIDIER ROBERT DE VAUGONDY, *Carte de la Virginie et du Maryland*, 1755

The first of a family of French cartographers, Didier Robert de Vaugondy (1723–86), served as Royal Geographer and Censor. This version of the Fry-Jefferson map is an elegant interpretation of the original work.

(opposite, above)

28. JEAN NICHOLAS BELLIN, *Carte de la Delaware Baye de Chesapeake*, 1757

A French cartographer interested in maritime subjects, Bellin published numerous maps relating to America's eastern coast.

(opposite)

29. THOMAS KITCHIN, *A Map of Maryland with the Delaware Counties and the Southern Part of New Jersey*, 1757

Kitchin, a prolific English publisher of the later eighteenth century, produced maps for a range of uses. The small-scale map, based on the Fry-Jefferson map, appeared within the *London Magazine* of August 1757.

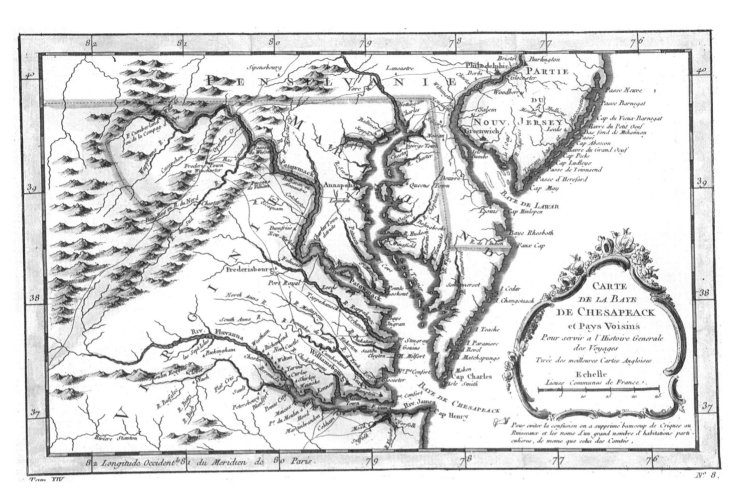

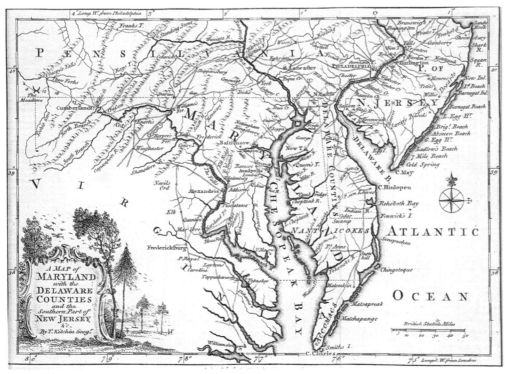

39

30. THOMAS JEFFERYS, *A Map of Virginia and Maryland*, [1770]

Serving as the geographer to King George III, Jefferys' work generally concentrated on British North America. Though being the king's geographer brought an elevated social status, no salary went with this honorific title, and Jefferys went bankrupt in 1768. This small scale copy of the Fry-Jefferson copy features an elaborate title cartouche.

31. W. THOMAS FISHER, [*Proposed Chesapeake-Delaware Canal Routes*], 1771

Fisher (1741–1810) uniquely combined an unrelated design for a machine devised for cutting files with an area map outlining prospective canal routes to produce this work.

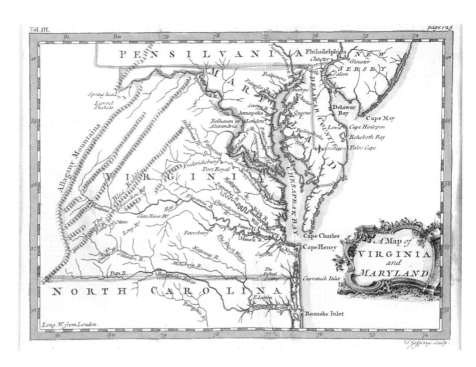

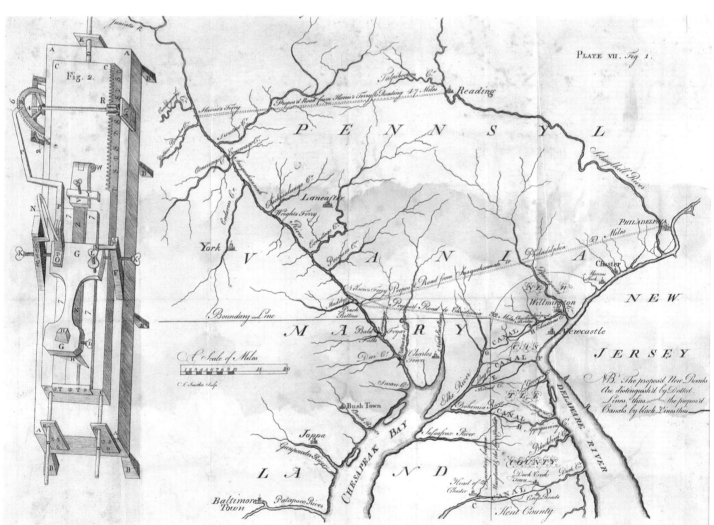

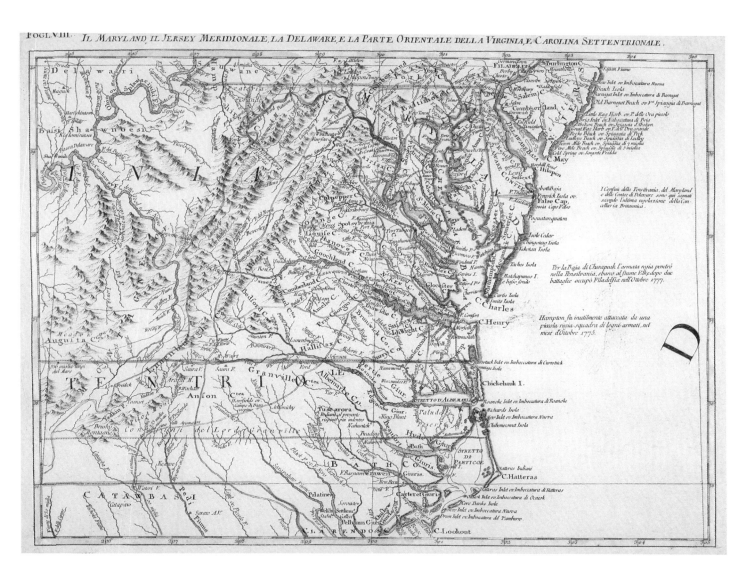

32. ROBERT SAYER & JOHN BENNET, *A General Map of the British Middle Colonies*, 1776

    (See color plate on page 22.)

33. GEORGES-LOUIS LE ROUGE, *Virginie, Maryland, en 2 feuilles par Fry et Jefferson*, 1777

    (See color plate on page 23.)

34. ANTONIO ZATTA, *Virginia, Maryland, Carolina*, 1778

    Zatta, a Venetian publisher, produced a series of maps that documented America at the time of the Revolutionary War. These elegant works often contained information concerning battles and lesser engagements relating to the conflict.

35.

JOHN HINTON (*Universal Magazine*),
*A New & Accurate Map of the Province
of Virginia in North America*, 1779

36.

JOHN HINTON (*Universal Magazine*),
*A New Map of the Province of
Maryland in North America*, 1780

English magazines for "Gentlemen"
often covered scientific and politi-
cal developments for their readers,
and sometimes included maps.

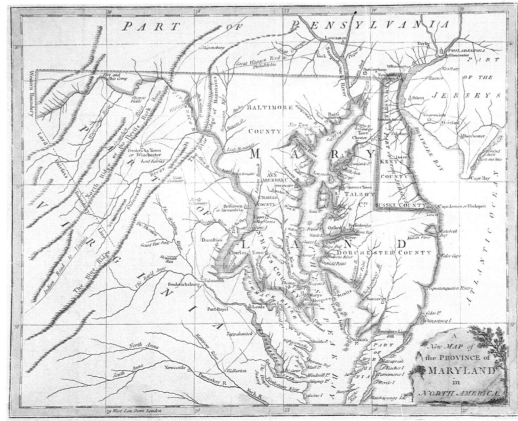

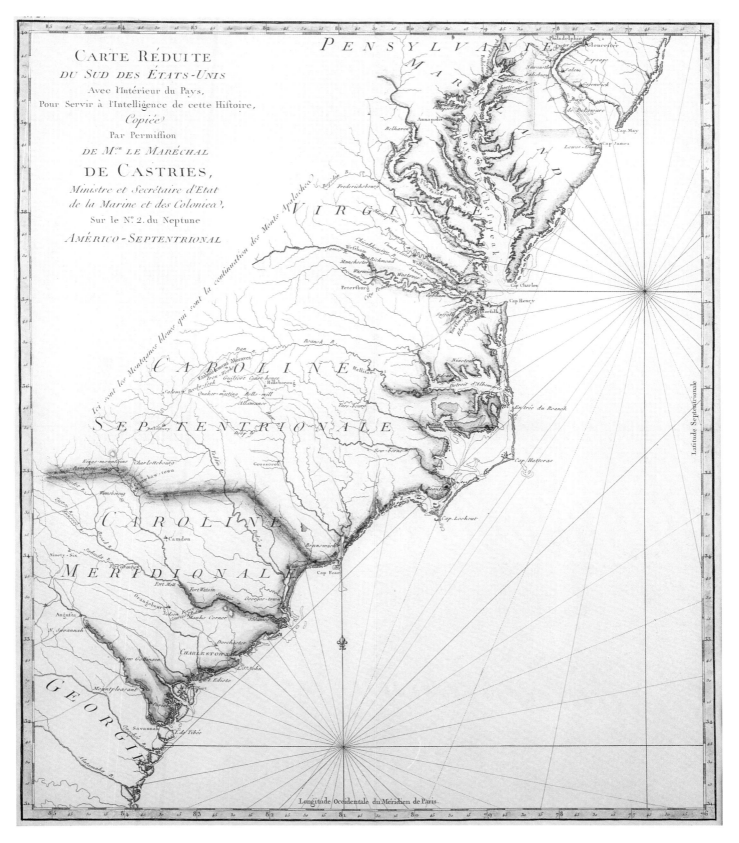

37. ODET-JULIEN LE BOUCHER, *Carte réduite du Sud des États-Unis*, 1787

Le Boucher (1744–1826) prepared this map of the southeastern United States for a French language
history of America's War of Independence entitled *Histoire de la dernière guerre, entre La Grande Bretagne et États Unis.*

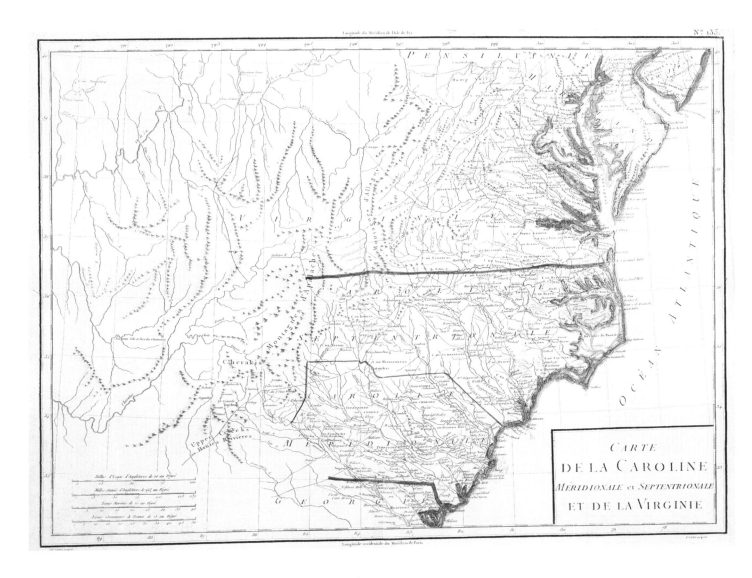

38. ANTOINE FRANCOIS TARDIEU, *Carte de la Caroline et de la Virginie*, 1787

An engraver and geographer, Tardieu (1757–1822) produced this map for another overview of the American Revolution. It appeared in Francois Soule's *Histoire des Troubles l'Amerique Anglois.*

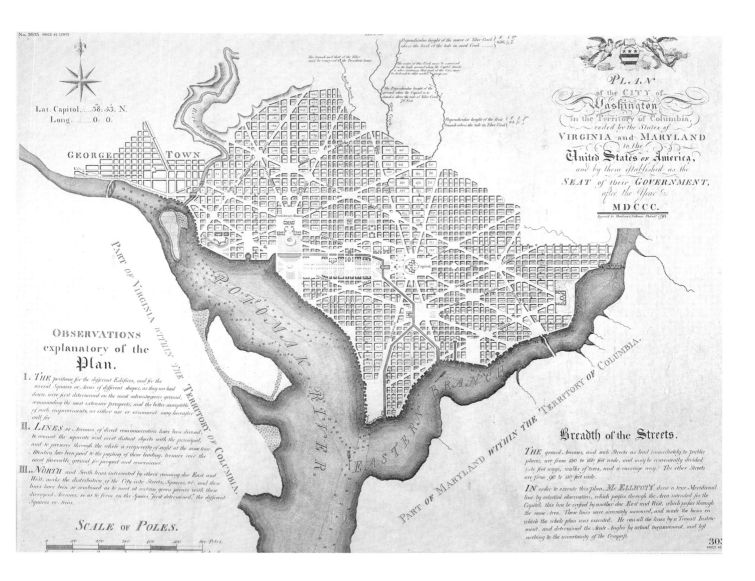

39. James Thackara & John Vallance, *Plan of the City of Washington*, 1792

Thackara and Vallance, Philadelpia engravers, produced this view of the Federal City based upon the survey of Andrew Ellicott and his assistant Benjamin Banneker. This map is a facsimile produced by the US Coast & Geodetic Survey in the late nineteenth century.

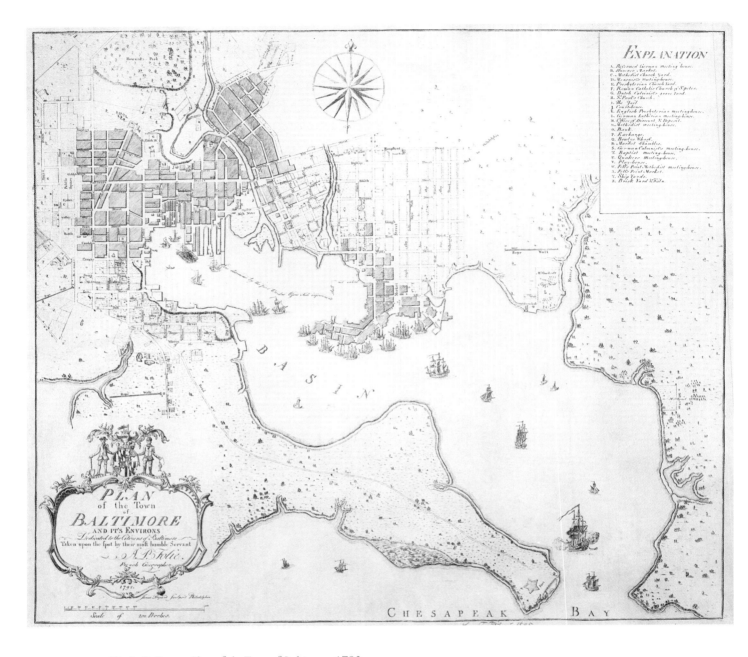

40. A. P. FOLIE, *Plan of the Town of Baltimore*, 1792

A. P. Folie, a French emigré from Santo Domingo, first settled in Philadelphia in the early 1790s. His map of Baltimore, funded by private subscription, is the earliest printed map of the city and its environs.

41. DENNIS GRIFFITH, *Map of the State of Maryland*, 1794 [1795]

(See color plate on pages 26 and 27.)

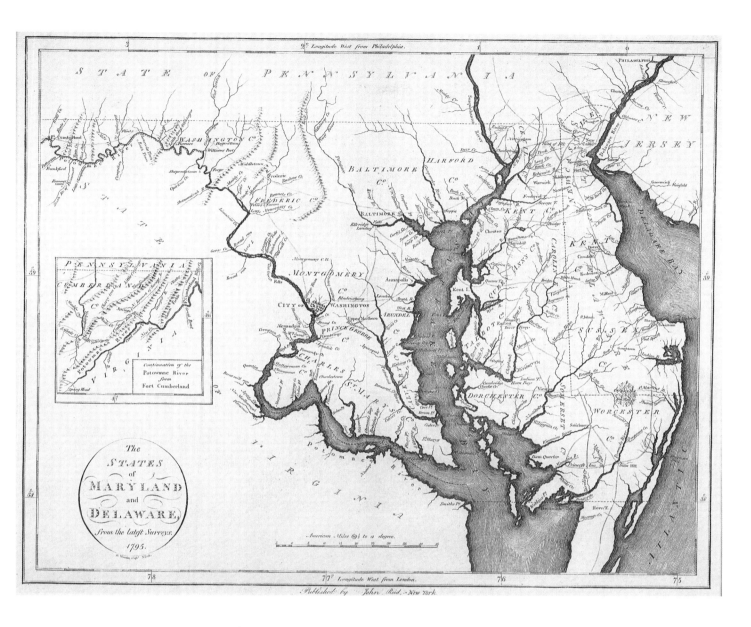

42. JOHN REID, *The States of Maryland and Delaware*,
1795 [1796] (second state)

A publisher based in New York, Reid included this
map in his *American Atlas*, one of the first general
atlases to be printed in the United States.

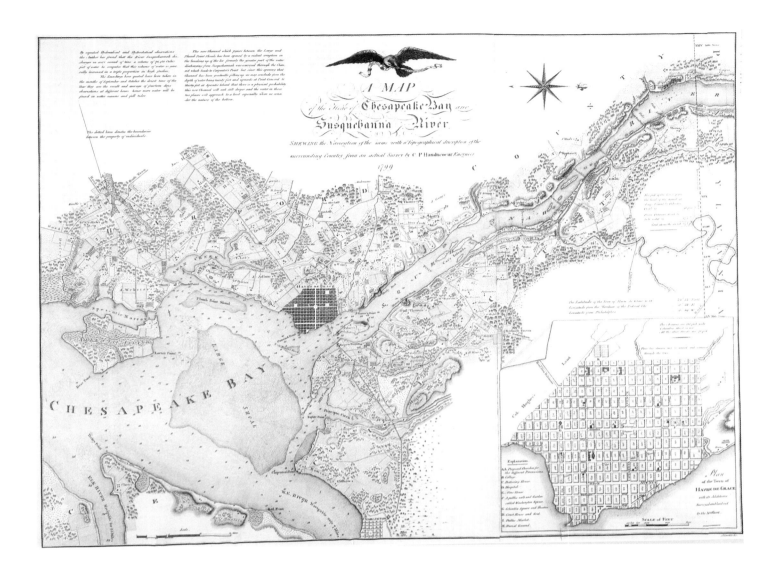

43. C. P. HAUDUCOEUR, *A Map of the Head of the Chesapeake Bay and Susquehanna River*, 1799

Hauducoeur produced this highly detailed map in order to induce investors to consider Havre de Grace as an alternative port to Baltimore.

(opposite, above)

44. [CHARLES VARLÉ], *Warner & Hanna's Plan of the City and Environs of Baltimore*, 1801

Charles P. Varlé, a French expatriate from Santo Domingo, settled in Maryland in 1798. Trained as an engineer, he contracted to prepare this early view of Baltimore for local publishers Warner & Hanna.

(opposite)

45. AARON ARROWSMITH, *Maryland*, 1804

Arrowsmith (1750–1833), an important English surveyor and cartographer, also served as hydrographer to the British monarch. He produced approximately two hundred maps, many large in scale, during the course of his career.

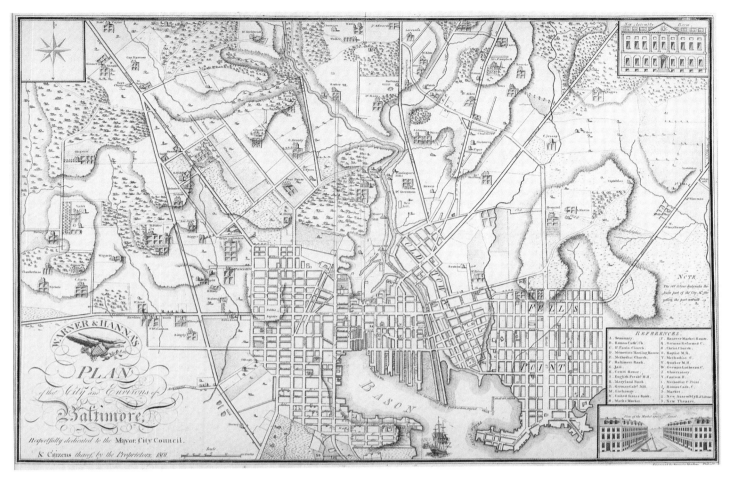

49

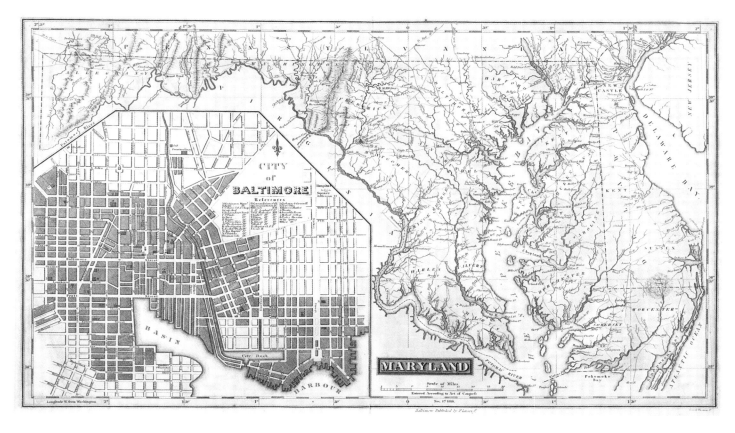

46. FIELDING LUCAS Jr., *Maryland*, 1819 [1824]

Lucas came to Baltimore in 1804 and involved himself in the selling of books, maps, and atlases. In 1811, he established his own business located on today's Baltimore Street, which continued after his death in 1854. This map is from Lucas's *Cabinet Atlas*, and is notable in that it contains the first urban plan, inset within the field of a larger map, to appear in any modern atlas.

47. JOHN MELISH, *Baltimore, Annapolis & Adjacent Counties*, 1822

Melish, a Scot working in Philadelphia and engaged primarily in the general map and atlas trade, produced this map for inclusion in his *Traveller's Dictionary Through the United States*.

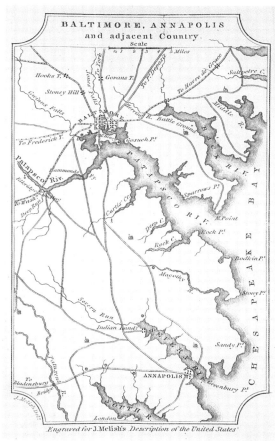

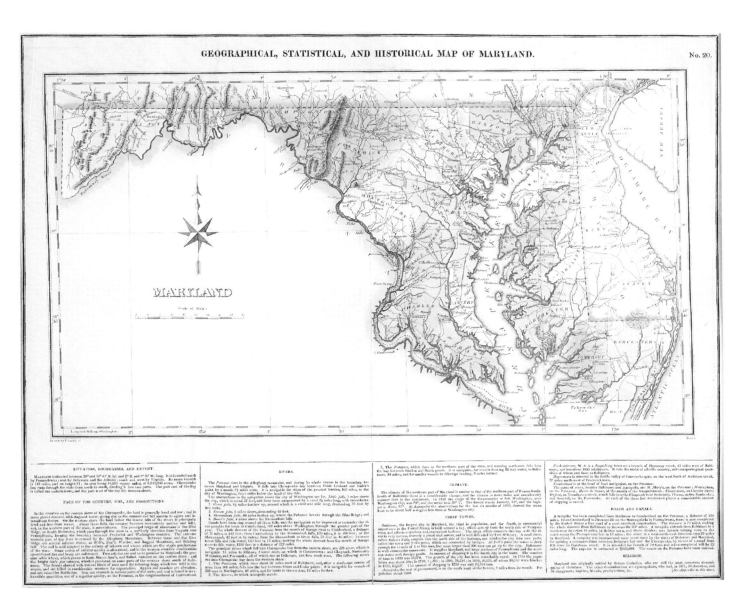

48. FIELDING LUCAS Jr., *Geographical, Statistical and Historical Map of Maryland*, 1822 [1823]

Lucas permitted Philadelphia publishers Carey and Lea to publish his 1819 map of Maryland minus its Baltimore inset. Contained within Carey's *Complete Historical, Chronological, and Geographical American Atlas*, this atlas is the first published in America to combine maps with descriptive text.

49. THOMAS H. POPPLETON, *Plan of the City of Baltimore*, 1822 [1852]

(See color plate on pages 28 and 29.)

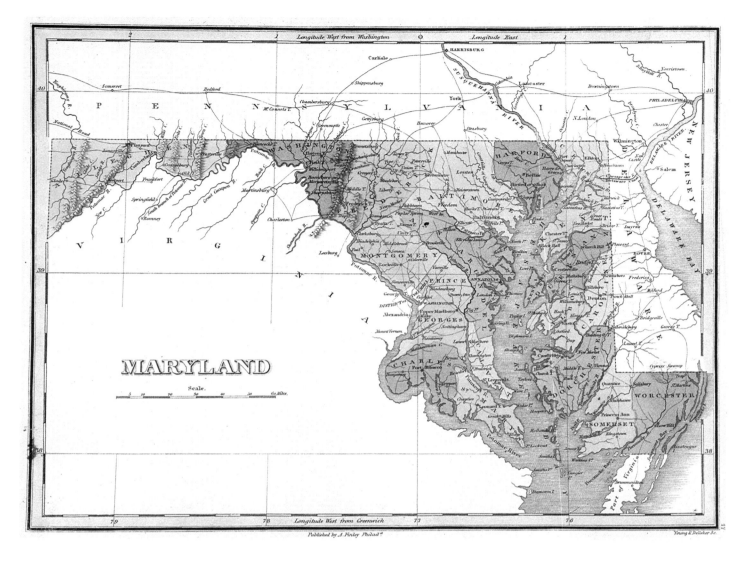

50. ANTHONY FINLEY, *Map of Virginia and Maryland*, 1824

Finley (c. 1790–1840), another Philadelphia publisher and cartographer, produced this map for inclusion in his *[N]ew American Atlas*.

(opposite, above)

51. S. BERNARD, *Map of Reconnaissance between Baltimore & Philadelphia*, [1827]

In May 1826, the U.S. Congress authorized a survey party to explore various new mail routes to Philadelphia. This map appeared as part of a government document the following year.

(opposite)

52. SIDNEY E MORSE, *Virginia, Maryland and Delaware*, 1828

Morse (1794–1871), publisher of a religious newspaper, expanded into map printing and in 1834 invented the wax engraving process (*cerography*), a technique soon to used widely by other map-makers. This view of the tri-state area appeared in Morse's *Universal Atlas*.

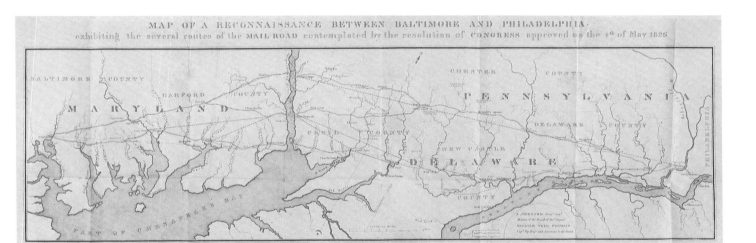

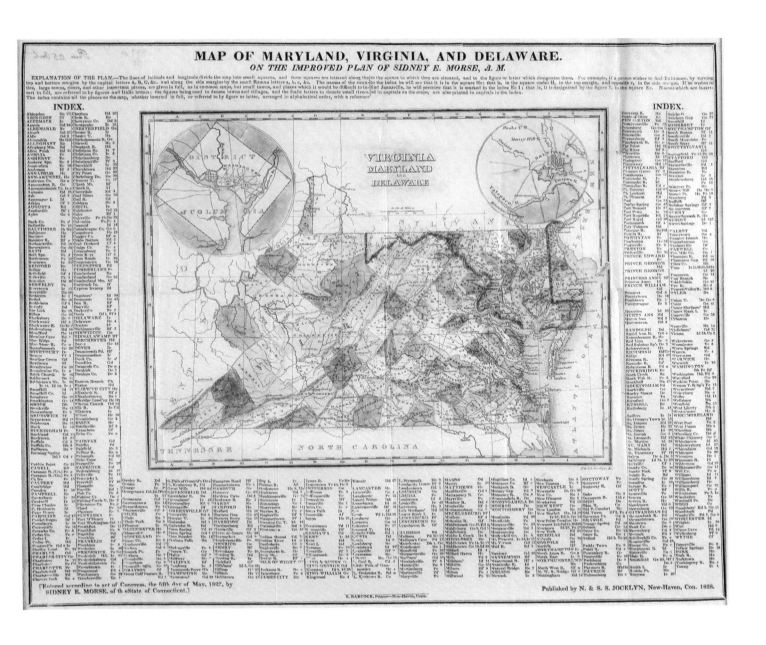

53

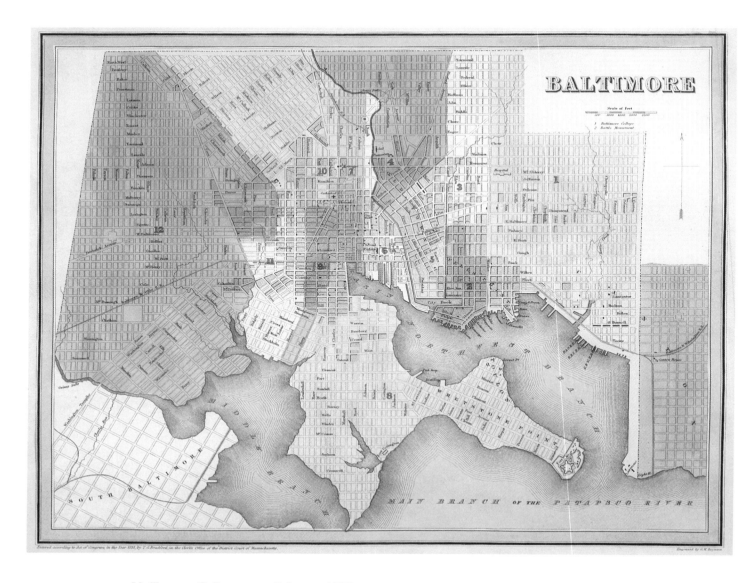

53. Thomas G. Bradford, *Baltimore*, 1838

Bradford produced this map for *An Illustrated atlas, geographical, statistical, and historical of the United States* (Philadelphia, 1838), one of the earliest atlases to incorporate folio-sized plans of both Baltimore and Maryland. Engraved by Boynton, this finely rendered work stands as one of the most aesthetically pleasing maps of nineteenth-century Baltimore.

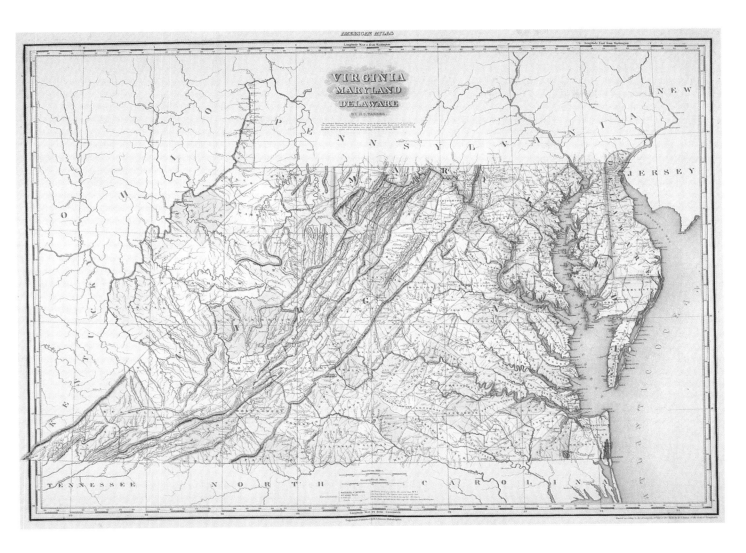

54. HENRY S. TANNER, *Virginia, Maryland and Delaware*, 1839

Working in Philadelphia as an engraver and publisher, Tanner prepared this regional map for inclusion in his *[N]ew American Atlas*. Tanner is considered to be one of the most prolific American mapmakers of the nineteenth century.

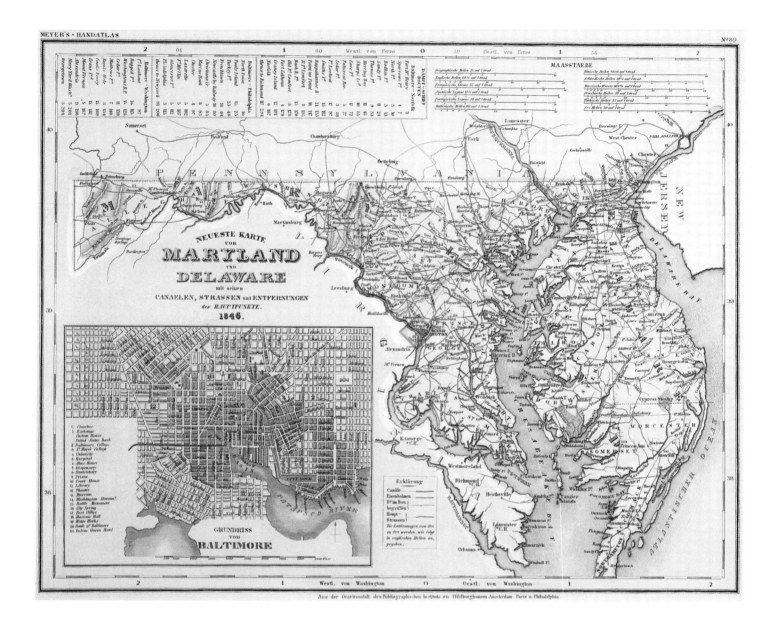

55. JOSEPH MEYER, *Maryland und Delaware*, 1846

Meyer, a German publisher, produced world and school atlases from the 1830s through the 1850s. This map of Baltimore, from his *Grosser Hand Atlas*, may have been studied by German emigrés before their departure to America. During the 1850s, Baltimore served as a major point of entry for Germans who had departed their homeland for the United States.

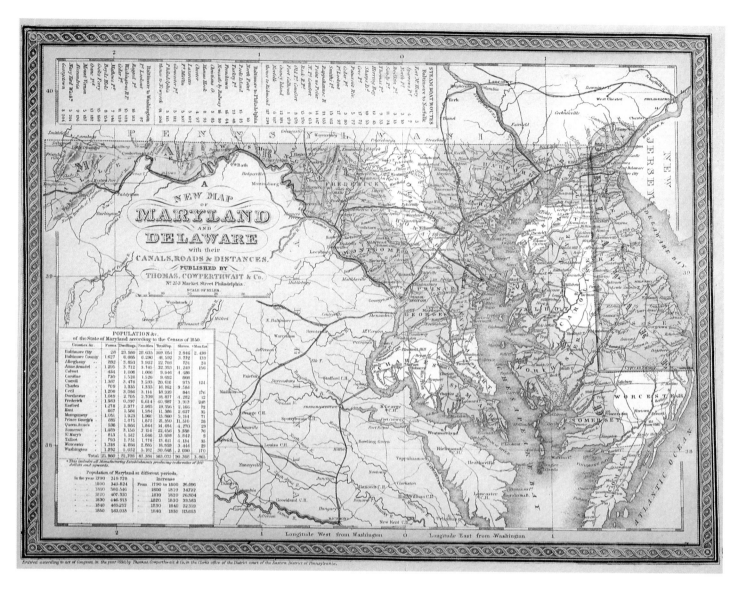

56. THOMAS, COWPERTHWAITE & CO., *A New Map of Maryland and Delaware*, 1850

The Philadelphia publishing house of Thomas, Cowperthwaite & Co. specialized in atlas publication.

58. JOSEPH HUTCHINS COLTON, *City of Baltimore*, 1855

Though lacking formal cartographical training, Colton produced a successful series of American maps and atlases for public consumption. Most of his maps focus on individual states or regions, but his company also produced world atlases. By 1850 the company's production emphasized guidebooks and railroad maps that aided new immigrants.

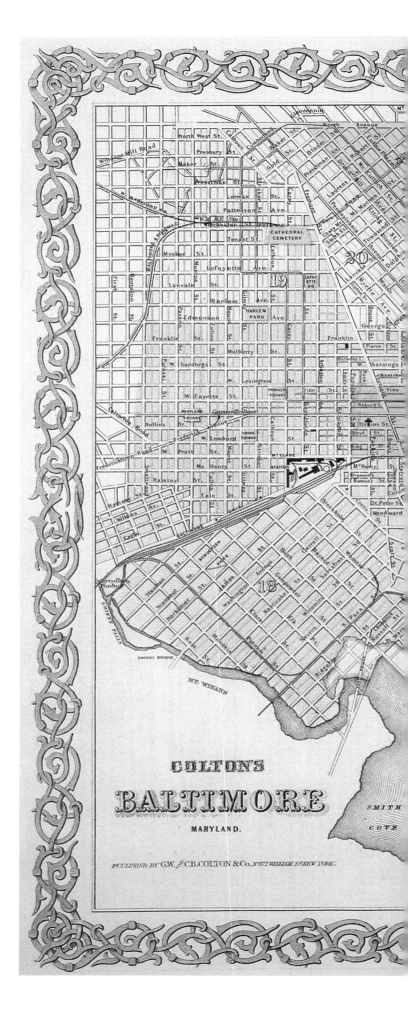

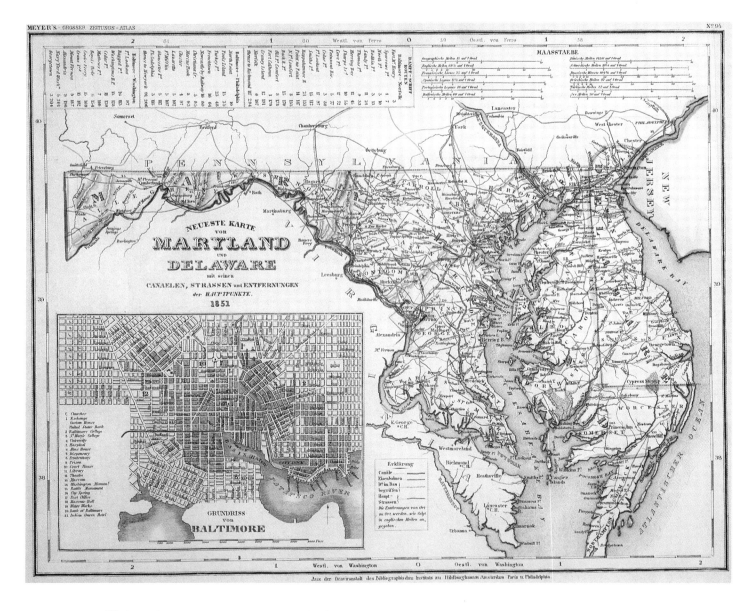

57. JOSEF MEYER, *Neuste Karte von Maryland
    und Delaware*, 1851

This work is a later edition of Meyer's 1846 map
(see plate 55). With the exception of the
European mileage comparison chart in the upper
right corner, the design of both maps can be
directly traced to Henry S. Tanner's *Maryland and
Delaware*, 1838.

59. S. Augustus Mitchell Jr., *Plan of Baltimore*, 1860
[1884]

The S. Augustus Mitchell publishing company of
Philadelphia was one of the dominant map produc-
ers of the nineteenth century. Mitchell's son took
the helm about 1860 and produced this view of
the Monumental City.

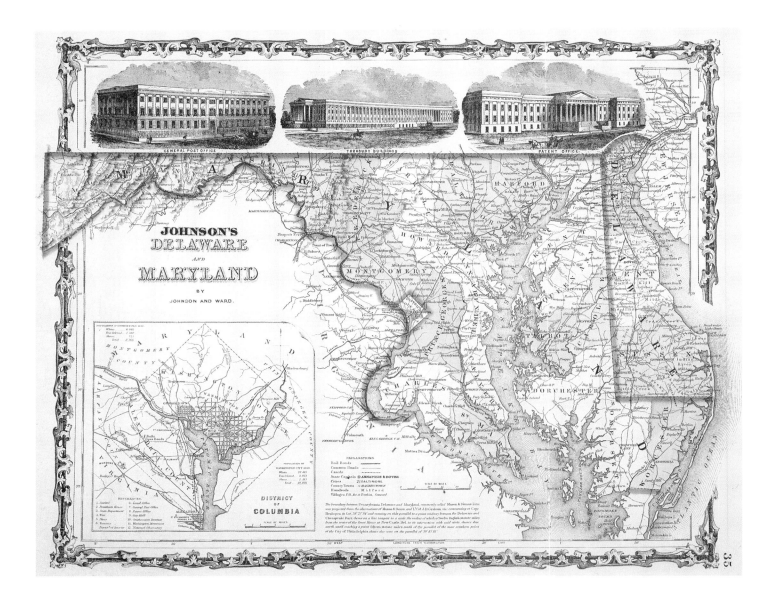

60. JOHNSON & WARD, *Johnson's Delaware and Maryland*, 1864

This decorative map, produced during the Civil War, contains vignettes of U.S. government buildings in Washington and an inset plan of that city.

61. O. W. GRAY & SON, *Gray's New Map of Baltimore*, 1876

The Philadelphia-based firm produced this map for inclusion within an atlas.

O. W. GRAY & SON, *Gray's New Map of Maryland*, 1876

(See color plate on pages 30 and 31.)

62. WILLIAM P. TWAMLEY [for the *Baltimore Sun*], *Map of the City of Baltimore*, 1882

(See color plate on pages 32.)

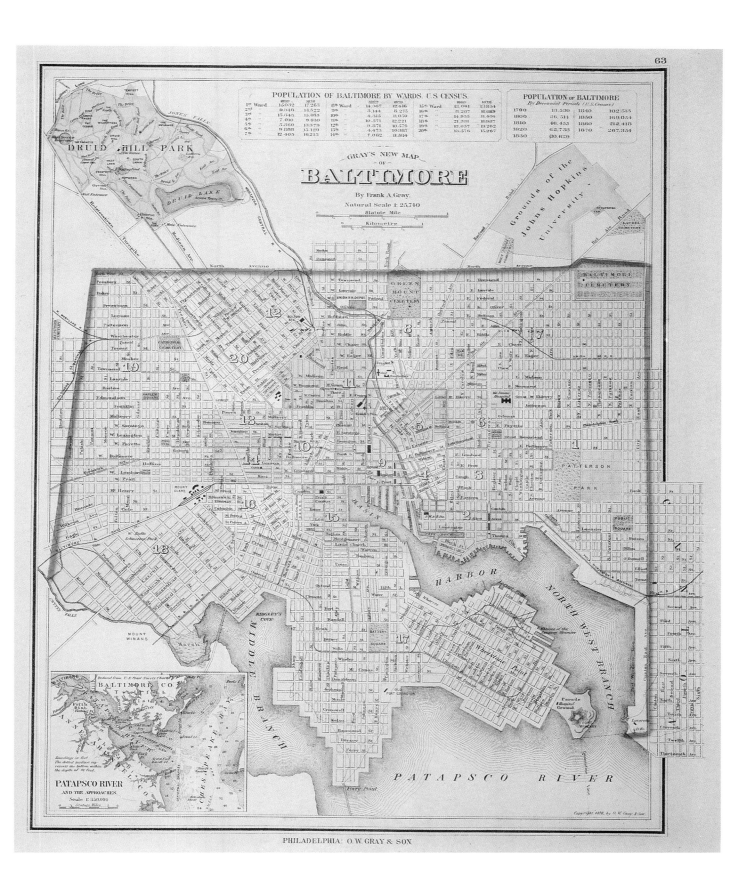

POPULATION OF BALTIMORE BY WARDS. U.S CENSUS.

Ward	1860	1870	Ward	1860	1870	Ward	1860	1870
1st Ward	15,032	17,263	8th Ward	14,367	12,416	15th Ward	13,061	13,854
2nd	9,740	14,522	9th	5,144	8,275	16th	8,267	16,689
3rd	15,545	13,483	10th	4,315	11,059	17th	14,955	11,404
4th	7,010	9,430	11th	10,571	12,221	18th	21,534	18,987
5th	5,860	13,379	12th	9,371	10,575	19th	13,057	13,262
6th	9,888	13,129	13th	4,473	10,367	20th	13,576	15,267
7th	12,405	16,215	14th	7,062	11,544			

POPULATION OF BALTIMORE
By Decennial Periods (U.S Census)

Year	Population	Year	Population
1790	13,530	1840	102,513
1800	26,514	1850	169,054
1810	46,455	1860	212,418
1820	62,738	1870	267,354
1830	80,620		

GRAY'S NEW MAP
OF
BALTIMORE
By Frank A. Gray.

Natural Scale 1: 25,740

Statute Mile

Kilometre

DRUID HILL PARK

DRUID LAKE

Grounds of the Johns Hopkins University

BALTIMORE CEMETERY

GREEN MOUNT CEMETERY

PATTERSON PARK

HARBOR

NORTH WEST BRANCH

MIDDLE BRANCH

PATAPSCO RIVER

BALTIMORE CO.

PATAPSCO RIVER
AND THE APPROACHES
Scale 1: 350,000

PHILADELPHIA: O. W. GRAY & SON

Letter of marque and Reprisal
Crew 30
Cargo main objective

Balto
122 commissioned vessel
78 L M + R
33 Captured
5 chased ashore
19 took enemy
merchant Ships

Barque frost
Undeclared war
with France
in Vigilant
1798 - 1800
fighting in West Indies

Comet
400,000 in earnings
35 vessels captured
3 cruises
9 made it to port
7 retaken
unsel destroyed
built 1810
Capt. Thorn dula
Chase - ow ot

Crew composite
1806: 1000 fm
Baltimn
1812 - 4,700 fm
Baltimn
crew fm
northern
ports
800, 17%
W & C African
American
Coggeshul
Dolphin
took 12 vassels
a 54,000

Designed by Gerard A. Valerio.
Bookmark Studio, Annapolis, Maryland.

Photography by Jeff Goldman,
Maryland Historical Society.

Composed in Perpetua by Sherri Ferritto,
Typeline, Annapolis.

Color separations, printing and binding
by Whitmore Print & Imaging,
Annapolis.